Norman Rockwell's World of Scouting

THE SCOUT OATH

On my honor I will do my best

To do my duty to God and my country
and to obey the Scout Law;

To help other people at all times;

To keep myself physically strong,
mentally awake, and morally straight.

THE SCOUT LAW

A SCOUT IS

TRUSTWORTHY. A Scout's honor is to be trusted. If he were to violate his honor by telling a lie, or by cheating, or by not doing exactly a given task, when trusted on his honor, he may be directed to hand over his Scout badge.

LOYAL. He is loyal to all to whom loyalty is due, his Scout leader, his home, and parents and country.

HELPFUL. He must be prepared at any time to save life, help injured persons, and share the home duties. He must do at least one Good Turn to somebody every day.

FRIENDLY. He is a friend to all and a brother to every other Scout.

COURTEOUS. He is polite to all, especially to women, children, old people and the weak and helpless. He must not take pay for being helpful or courteous.

KIND. He is a friend to animals. He will not kill nor hurt any living creature needlessly, but will strive to save and protect all harmless life.

OBEDIENT. He obeys his parents, Scoutmaster, patrol leader, and all other duly constituted authorities.

CHEERFUL. He smiles whenever he can. His obedience to orders is prompt and cheery. He never shirks nor grumbles at hardships.

THRIFTY. He does not wantonly destroy property. He works faithfully, wastes nothing, and makes the best use of his opportunities. He saves his money so that he may pay his own way, be generous to those in need, and helpful to worthy objects. He may work for pay, but must not receive tips for courtesies or Good Turns.

BRAVE. He has the courage to face danger in spite of fear, and to stand up for the right against the coaxings of friends or the jeers or threats of enemies, and defeat does not down him.

CLEAN. He keeps clean in body and thought, stands for clean speech, clean sport, clean habits, and travels with a clean crowd.

REVERENT. He is reverent toward God. He is faithful in his religious duties, and respects the convictions of others in matters of custom and religion.

William Hillcourt

Norman Rockwell's

World of

Scouting

A Fireside Book
Published by Simon and Schuster
New York

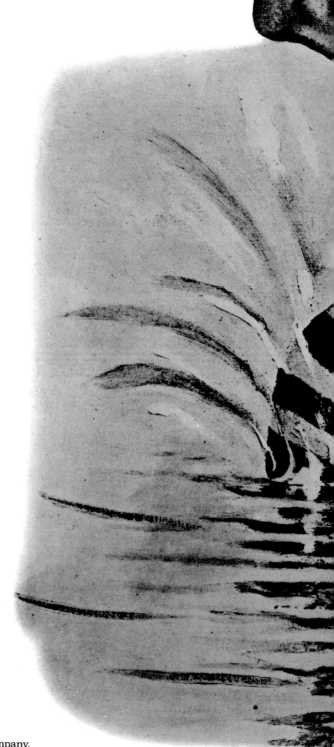

Darlene Geis, *Editor*

Patricia Gilchrest, *Associate Editor*

Dirk Luykx, *Designer*

Text and reproductins of works of art only
Copyright © 1977 by Harry N. Abrams, Inc.
All rights reserved
including the right of reproduction
in whole or in part in any form
First Fireside Edition, 1980
Published by Simon and Schuster
A Division of Gulf & Western Corporation
Simon & Schuster Building
Rockefeller Center
1230 Avenue of the Americas
New York, New York 10020
FIRESIDE and colophon are trademarks
of Simon & Schuster
Manufactured in the United States of America

1 2 3 4 5 6 7 8 9 10

Library of Congress Cataloging in Publication Data

Hillcourt, William, date.
    Norman Rockwell's world of scouting.

    (A Fireside book)
    Includes index.
    1. Rockwell, Norman, 1894-1978. 2. Boy
Scouts of America in art. 3. Boy Scouts of America
—History. I. Rockwell, Norman 1894-1978.
II. Title.
[ND237.R68H54   1980]   759.13   80-20293
ISBN 0-671-41232-9 Pbk.

Contents

Norman PRockwell

Acknowledgments

10

The author's thanks go to the following people for their help: Norman and Thomas Rockwell for biographical incidents in their book *Norman Rockwell—My Adventures As an Illustrator;* for personal assistance: Claire V. Fry and M.W. Eichers, former and present Creative Directors of Brown & Bigelow for

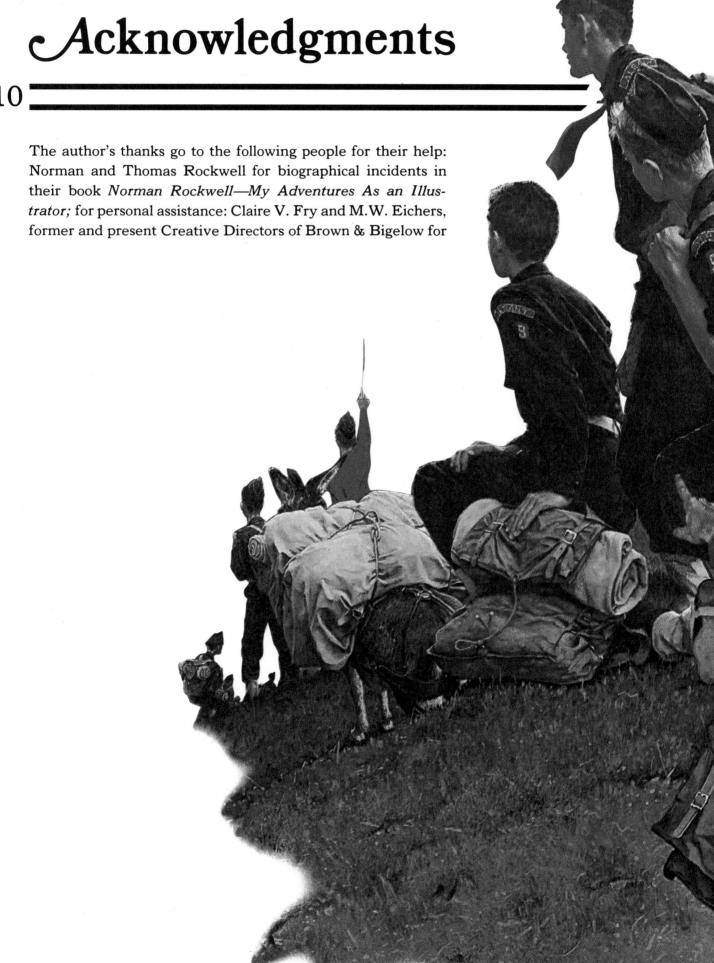

details about Rockwell's calendar paintings; Donald Ross, Marshall Ammerman, Norman Mathiews, Keith Monroe, Dr. Robert West, Joseph Csatari, and Dominick Spilatro for anecdotes and photographs; Grace Hillcourt for having held on to Norman's circus sketch, given her by her boss, James E. West; and most of all to Darlene Geis for encouragement and valuable cooperation, and Dirk Luykx for his imaginative layouts.

Thanks also to the Boy Scouts of America and Brown & Bigelow for making the Rockwell Boy Scout paintings available, and particularly to Avery Chenoweth, Director, Audio-Visual Division of the Boy Scouts, and Ilmar Pleer, Manager of the Johnston Historical Scouting Museum, for their special assistance.

W.H.

THE SCOUTING TRAIL

This is the Trail that the Scout shall know
Where knightly qualities thrive and grow;
The trail of honor and truth and worth
And the strength that springs from the
      good brown earth;
The trail that Scouts, in their seeking, blaze
Through the toughest tangle, the deepest maze,
Till out of Boyhood the Scout comes straight
To Manhood's splendid and high estate!

Introduction

O n a bright fall day in 1912, a young artist got off the elevator on the eighth floor of New York's Fifth Avenue Building. He looked around for the entrance he was seeking, found it and walked into the national office of the Boy Scouts of America.

"I should like to see the editor of *Boys' Life* magazine," he said.

"His name is Mr. Edward Cave," said the receptionist. "His office is the first door to your left."

The young artist followed the instructions. He found the door marked *Boys' Life* and knocked on it. Someone said "Come in!"

The young man entered, introduced himself, and got right to business.

"I understand that you will be needing some artists to illustrate stories for your magazine. I would like you to see what I can do."

The artist opened up his portfolio and began to exhibit his wares. He spread out some of the illustrations he had made under the guidance of his teacher at the Art Students League.

The young artist, whose illustrations set him on The Scouting Trail himself in 1912, became one of the foremost interpreters of the Boy Scouts' activities and ideals. By 1939, when this was painted, he had mastered not only his craft but all of the intricacies and fine points of Scouting equipment and uniforms as worn by Cub Scout, Scout, and Sea Scout.

THE SCOUTING TRAIL 1939

He showed off a children's book he had illustrated. He opened a historical book to a charcoal frontispiece he had made. He displayed some pen-and-ink Christmas cards he had designed.

The editor seemed impressed.

"How old are you?" he wanted to know.

The young artist admitted to eighteen years.

"You appear to be quite qualified for the kind of art work I should like to have done," Cave said.

"Here is a story by Stanley Snow. You may have heard of him—he is quite a well-known writer of stories for boys. You might try your hand at illustrating it. Pick three incidents and let us have some charcoals of them. And, incidentally," he added, "I have just completed the manuscript for a book of my own for Boy Scouts on hiking and overnight camping. Your style of pen-and-ink sketching may be just right for the illustrations. Take along a couple of chapters and let me see how you would illustrate them."

The young artist was jubilant when he left. He held in his hand his first commission for a magazine job, and another commission for illustrating a book that might become very popular.

Thus began the career of Norman Rockwell—a career that eventually made him, through his art, the spokesman for Scouting, its program and its ideals.

A career, also, that brought him fame and fortune as the beloved interpreter of the mores and spirit of twentieth-century America.

The Birth of Scouting

CHIEF SCOUT OF THE WORLD

The Scout Movement was founded by a brilliant Englishman, one of the most effective champions of boyhood who has ever lived—Lord Baden-Powell of Gilwell, affectionately known to all Scouts as "B-P" and proclaimed "Chief Scout of the World" by the Scouts of all nations.

Robert Stephenson Smyth Baden-Powell was born in London, England, on February 22, 1857, the seventh son and twelfth child of the Rev. Baden Powell, professor at Oxford University. His mother, Henrietta Grace Smyth, was the daughter of the British admiral William Henry Smyth.

Robert's father died when he was only three years old, leaving his mother to raise the seven children still living at home. Robert lived a glorious outdoor life with his four brothers, hiking and camping with them in many parts of England, paddling the Thames river by canoe and boating along the Channel coast.

In 1870 Baden-Powell entered Charterhouse School in London on a scholarship. He was not an especially outstanding scholar, but was certainly one of the liveliest. His dramatic

Robert Baden-Powell became Chief Scout of the World in 1920 and was further honored for his Boy Scout work in 1929, when King George V conferred a peerage on him. This portrait, painted by Harold N. Anderson, shows him in Scout uniform, wearing his decorations as well as the Silver Buffalo and Bronze Wolf. He is carrying a thumb stick of his own design, the three prongs representing the three parts of the original British Scout oath. The portrait is framed by the fleur-de-lis badge of the Scouts. The badge, designed by Baden-Powell, was based on the arrowhead that points north on a mariner's compass.

abilities were highly appreciated by his fellow students, and he was also artistically inclined—his gift for sketching later made it possible for him to illustrate his own writings.

Soon after Baden-Powell entered Charterhouse, the school was moved out of London to Godalming in Surrey, to a location that included an untouched belt of woodland wilderness. Although this area was out of bounds to the pupils, Robert managed to use "The Copse," as it was called, in his early outdoor training. Here he taught himself to snare rabbits and cook them over a fire so tiny that the smoke would not give him away to a prowling tutor. He also learned tracking and stalking—two skills that would prove important to him in his future life.

The year that young Baden-Powell graduated from Charterhouse—1876—Queen Victoria was proclaimed Empress of India. The British Army needed more officers for its overseas forces and at the age of nineteen, he shipped off to India as a sub-lieutenant, to join the regiment that had formed the right end of the cavalry line in the famous "Charge of the Light Brigade" in the Crimean War.

Besides performing excellent military service—he was a captain at the age of twenty-six—Baden-Powell won the most desired sports trophy in all India, that for "pigsticking," wild-boar hunting on horseback with a short lance as the only

The tricks of evading a prowling tutor that Baden-Powell learned in "The Copse" of Charterhouse were the same ones he used later in some of his military exploits.

The twenty-six-year-old captain served in India with distinction. He made this drawing of the dangerous sport called "pig-sticking" from firsthand experience, having won a trophy as a champion hunter of wild boar.

weapon. The danger of this sport can be best appreciated from the fact that the wild boar is often referred to as "the only animal that dares drink at the same water hole with a tiger."

After eight years' service in India, Baden-Powell returned with his regiment to England. During the next two years, 1885 to

The Zulu chief Dinizulu, fleeing the British forces, left behind a necklace consisting of hundreds of tiny wooden beads. When Baden-Powell established an advanced Scoutmastership course in 1919, he awarded two of Dinizulu's beads to each trainee. The course, thereafter, became known as "Wood Badge," and specially trained Scoutmasters to this day wear "Dinizulu's beads" in replica.

In the watercolor at left Baden-Powell expressed his concern about the future of South Africa: "Will a proud Zulu warrior be satisfied with a life as a mine worker?"

In one of his military sketches (below) Baden-Powell concealed the outline of a fortress in the wings of a butterfly. The marks on the wings between the lines mean nothing, but those on the lines show the nature and size of the guns, according to the key below.

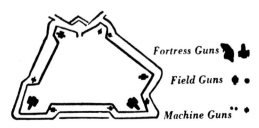

Fortress Guns

Field Guns

Machine Guns

1886, he had the chance to travel on secret missions around Europe.

His next assignment was service in Africa. Shortly after his arrival in Cape Town, one of the Zulu tribes to the north rose in rebellion against the British. Baden-Powell was appointed staff officer for the forces sent in to suppress the uprising. The rebellious Zulu chief, Dinizulu, fled the area into the neighboring independent Republic of Transvaal where he could not be pursued, and order was restored.

In 1890 Baden-Powell's uncle, Sir Henry Smyth, became commander-in-chief of the British forces and governor of the Mediterranean island of Malta. He invited his nephew, recently promoted to brevet major, to join him as military secretary and aide-de-camp. Robert accepted with alacrity and enjoyed three pleasant years on Malta.

During this period he acted as intelligence officer for the whole Mediterranean area, an assignment that enabled him to use some of his special abilities on missions into Austria, Italy, Albania, and Turkey. He displayed an uncanny skill in disguising himself and in acting the part: an artist painting an Alpine sunrise in an area where Italian troops were on maneuver, or perhaps a lepidopterist hunting butterflies around a Dalmatian fortification. If stopped by anyone, he flourished his sketchbook and was soon set free. The arresting officers had no way of knowing that the innocent-looking drawing of a mountain ridge showed the positions of army units, or that the design of a butterfly wing contained the outline of a fortification and the locations of its guns.

The boys of Mafeking were formed into a cadet corps to carry military messages, deliver civilian mail, and act as orderlies. Baden-Powell was amazed at the eagerness with which the boys accepted responsibility and the thoroughness and lack of fear with which they carried out their assigned tasks.

After finishing his Malta tour, Baden-Powell served in Africa. Because of his courage, his uncanny scouting skills, and his amazing tracking abilities, the natives feared him so much that they gave him the name of "Impeesa"—"the Wolf That Never Sleeps."

Baden-Powell's advancements in rank were almost automatic, so regularly did they occur—until suddenly he achieved world fame. It was the year 1899, and he had risen to the rank of colonel.

Trouble was brewing in South Africa. War with the Boers seemed inevitable. Baden-Powell was directed to proceed to Rhodesia, raise two regiments of mounted infantry and secure the area around Mafeking, a small town but an important railroad center in the heart of South Africa. "Who holds Mafeking, holds the reins of South Africa," a popular saying, proved to be true.

War came. For 217 days Baden-Powell held Mafeking, though besieged by overwhelming numbers of the enemy, until relief forces finally fought their way to him on May 17, 1900.

After the lifting of the siege of Mafeking, Baden-Powell was given the job of organizing a South African constabulary "to act as a police . . . for preserving the peace and preventing crimes." He wrote a manual of instruction for the men and designed their uniform, including a broad-brimmed hat.

The British Army had gone from defeat to defeat during the South African campaign. The only bright spot had been Baden-Powell's holding of Mafeking. When finally the news came, "Mafeking has been relieved!" the whole British Empire went mad with joy. Look up "maffick" in the dictionary and you will find it means "to celebrate with boisterous rejoicing," a word created on that wild victory night, "Mafeking Night," from the name of the African town.

Baden-Powell, raised to the rank of major-general by Queen Victoria, found himself a hero in the eyes of his countrymen.

When he returned to England in 1901, he was showered with honors and discovered to his amazement that as a result of his personal popularity *Aids to Scouting,* his book for army men, had become extremely popular. It was being used as a textbook in boys' schools.

Baden-Powell saw a great challenge in this. He realized that here was his opportunity to help the boys of his country grow into strong manhood. If a book for men on military scouting practices could appeal to boys and inspire them, how much more appealing would be a book written for the boys themselves!

He set to work adapting his boyhood adventures with his brothers, his experiences in India and among the tribes of Africa. He read of the training of boys throughout the ages—the Spartan boys, the ancient British, the American Indians, the African Zulus, the youth organizations of his own day.

Slowly and carefully, Baden-Powell developed the Scouting idea. He wanted to be sure that it would work, so in the summer of 1907 he took a group of twenty-two boys with him to the island of Brownsea in Poole Harbor on the southern coast of

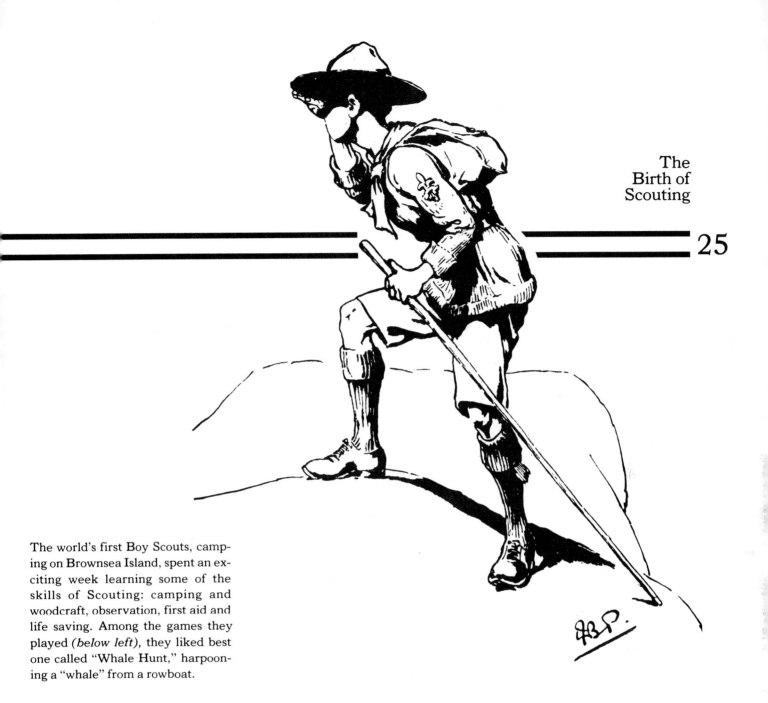

The world's first Boy Scouts, camping on Brownsea Island, spent an exciting week learning some of the skills of Scouting: camping and woodcraft, observation, first aid and life saving. Among the games they played *(below left)*, they liked best one called "Whale Hunt," harpooning a "whale" from a rowboat.

England, for the first Boy Scout camp the world had ever seen. The camp was a great success.

And then, in the early months of 1908, he brought out, in six fortnightly parts, his *Scouting for Boys,* a handbook for training illustrated by himself, never dreaming that this book would set in motion a movement that was to affect the boys of the entire world.

His book challenged boys to better citizenship. It told them how to live an adventuresome life in the outdoors, how to hike and camp, how to grow physically strong. It advised them on forming patrols, on picking their own boy leaders and doing real Scouting. It showed them pictures of a special uniform to wear, of badges to earn. It held before them a code of honor—a Scout Law and a Scout Promise of high resolve—and charged them to help other people at all times, to "Do a Good Turn Daily."

By 1910 the Scout movement had reached such proportions that Baden-Powell realized Scouting was to be his life work. He had the vision and faith to recognize that he could do more for his country by training the rising generation of boys to be good citizens than by training a few men for possible future fighting.

And so he resigned from the British Army where he had become a lieutenant general and embarked upon his "second life," as he called it, his life of service to the world through Scouting.

He reaped his reward in the growth of the Scout movement and in the love and respect of boys around the globe.

The Scout movement spread around the world with astonishing speed—first throughout the British Empire, next to South America, where Baden-Powell vacationed in 1909, then to the United States and most of the countries of Europe. It eventually became the most widely accepted movement in the world for the training of youth for citizenship. Today, Scouting is practiced in more than one hundred countries around the globe.

Scouting
Comes to
America

It was a Good Turn that brought Scouting to the United States.

One day in the fall of 1909, the city of London was in the grip of a dense fog. An American publisher, William D. Boyce of Chicago, stopped under a street lamp to get his bearings. Out of the gloom a boy approached him and asked if he could be of help. Boyce gladly accepted the offer. He told the boy that he wanted to find a certain business office in the center of the city.

"I'll take you there," said the boy.

When they reached the destination, the American put his hand in his pocket for a tip. The boy quickly stopped him.

"No, thank you, sir," he said. "Not for doing a good turn."

"And why not?"

"Because I am a Scout. And a Scout doesn't take anything for helping."

"A Scout? And what might that be?" Boyce asked.

And so, the English boy told the American about himself and his brother Scouts. Boyce was interested in what he heard. After finishing his errand, he had the boy take him to the British Boy Scout office.

There the boy saluted and disappeared.

At the headquarters Boyce met Robert Baden-Powell, the famous British general who had founded the Scout movement

In one of his first Scout paintings, *The Daily Good Turn,* Norman Rockwell used the theme of the "Unknown Scout" doing his Good Turn for William D. Boyce. But he transferred the action from a foggy day in London to a cold evening in New York—to a street in 1918 with nary a car in sight!

The early, military-looking Scout uniform was transformed over the years into a more suitable field uniform. But no changes were made in the Scout Oath, which the Boy Scout of 1910, an Honor Badge winner, shares and holds with the Eagle Scout of fifty years later. By 1960, the younger branch—the Cub Scouts—had almost as many members as the Boy Scouts.
EVER ONWARD 1960

two years before. Boyce was so impressed with what he learned about Scouting that he decided to bring it home with him.

And so, on February 8, 1910, in Washington, D.C., Boyce and a group of other outstanding Americans interested in the welfare of boys incorporated the Boy Scouts of America. Ever since, this day has been observed as the birthday of American Scouting.

In the British Scout Training Center at Gilwell Park, England, there stands a beautiful statuette of an American buffalo. It represents the highest award of the Boy Scouts of America, the "Silver Buffalo," given for outstanding service to boyhood. It was put up in 1926 in honor of the "Unknown Scout" whose good turn brought the Scout movement to the United States.

Although one of Boyce's original intentions had been to use Scouting in the promotion of his Chicago publications, he quickly realized that the Scout idea was broader in scope than he had anticipated.

When, therefore, a group of outstanding American youth leaders, led by Edgar M. Robinson, secretary of the Committee on Boys' Work of the Young Men's Christian Association, approached him, he was willing to listen to their suggestions. They recommended calling together a group of prominent Americans with experience in boys' work for the purpose of creating a national Scout movement.

The meeting convened on June 21, 1910. As a result of this meeting, a special Committee on Organization was formed to proceed with the establishment of the Boy Scouts of America. Within the next three months, this committee managed to bring into the new movement other boys' groups as well as Boy Scout units that had sprung up in different parts of the country. It also formulated a set of bylaws and recruited a number of outstanding citizens to give their names, prestige, and efforts to the new movement.

In October, its work done, the Committee on Organization

turned its records and holdings over to a newly elected board of managers. Colin H. Livingston of Washington, D.C., who with Boyce had been one of the original incorporators, was elected the first President of the Boy Scouts of America. Ernest Thompson Seton became the first Chief Scout, and Daniel Carter Beard a National Scout Commissioner. To direct the work, the board of managers—soon renamed the executive board—picked a thirty-four-year-old Washington attorney named James E. West.

Curiously enough, of the three persons chosen to carry forward the Boy Scouts of America, two of them—Seton and Beard— like Baden-Powell, were both prominent author-artists.

Ernest Thompson Seton was born in 1860 in South Shields, Durham, England, the eighth of ten sons of a Scottish ship-owner. In 1866 the family emigrated to Canada. Here, in the primitive backwoods around Lindsay, Ontario, Seton came to know and love the wild animals and began making sketches of them and writing about their lives. When he was nineteen his father sent him to London and Paris to study art.

He returned to Canada in 1881 and became naturalist for the provincial government of Manitoba. Almost immediately, a steady stream of illustrated articles about North American wildlife began to flow from his pen. Seton made up his mind to make writing and illustrating his lifework.

In 1883 he took off for New York. He knew it was here that he would have his greatest chance of success. Soon after, his animal stories made their appearance in a wide range of American magazines.

In 1898 Charles Scribner's Sons published Seton's first book, *Wild Animals I Have Known*. It was illustrated by more than two hundred of the marginal pen-and-ink sketches that became a Seton trademark. The book was an instantaneous and substantial hit. It was followed by the equally successful *Biography of a Grizzly* and *Lives of the Hunted*.

Ernest Thompson Seton, the first Chief Scout of the Boy Scouts of America, was six feet tall, spare, sinewy, and athletic, with a shock of unruly hair and a bushy mustache. In his early books he created a gallery of highly popular animal characters: Lobo the Wolf, Tito the Coyote, Johnny the Bear, the Sandhill Stag, and many others. This portrait was painted in 1945 by Winfred Scott.

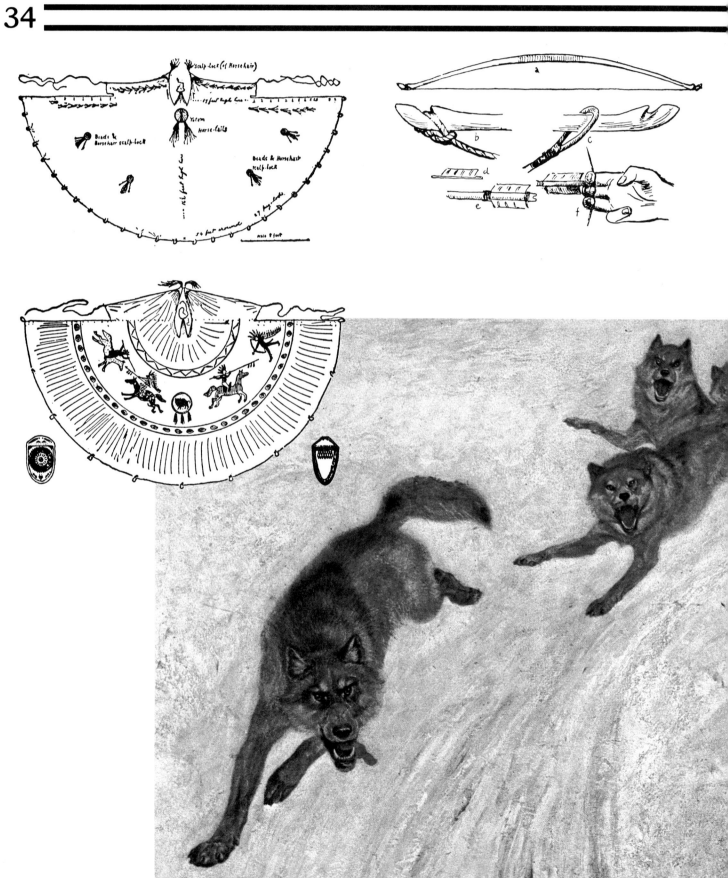

Spring soon

Spring com-ing

Some scientific naturalists of the day criticized Seton and other popular nature authors for their "humanizing" of animals and labeled them "nature fakers." Seton proved how wrong they were in his case by bringing out, in 1910, his two large quarto volumes *Life Histories of Northern Animals*. The work is a serious and reliable study, with meticulous illustrations by the author.

Because of the great appeal of Seton's writings to young readers, the *Ladies' Home Journal* asked him to prepare a series of articles for a new department on American woodcraft for boys. The first of these articles, entitled "Ernest Thompson Seton's Boys," appeared in the magazine in May 1902.

Numerous requests arrived at the office of the magazine for reprints of the seven articles he had written. Seton accommodated his readers by collecting the articles into a pamphlet, *How to Play Injun*. Finally, in 1906, the publishers of his nature books brought out his material in book form under the title *The Birch-Bark Roll of the Woodcraft Indians*.

His efforts in working with boys had resulted in a loosely knit organization of "Woodcraft Indians," with a program of Indian lore and a code based on Indian tribal laws.

But Seton had other abilities beyond being a writer and illustrator. He was a magnificent speaker with an almost overwhelming personality. He could grasp and hold an audience and could make young and old enthusiastic about his cause.

He was a logical choice for the first Chief Scout of the Boy Scouts of America.

Daniel Carter Beard was born in Ohio in 1850, when Cincinnati was still the gateway to an unexplored West, when covered wagons, pulled by teams of slow-moving oxen, frequently passed his home.

Soon after his birth, the family moved to Kentucky—a territory abounding in legends of Daniel Boone. Here the boy had a chance to roam the wilderness, to paddle a canoe on lakes and streams, to learn about animals and birds, to pick up the skills of the early American pioneers.

The entire Beard family was artistically inclined. Daniel's father, his three older brothers, and his uncle were all excellent draftsmen. They encouraged the boy to draw and sketch. In his teens he applied his abilities as a draftsman to the study of engineering. In 1869, at the age of nineteen, he graduated as a full-fledged engineer and surveyor.

Beard then went to New York where he became a draftsman for the Sanborn Map Company. But he changed his direction soon afterwards. While he was visiting his brother Frank's designing and engraving studio, the art editor of *St. Nicholas* magazine arrived with a commission for Frank and was shown some of Dan's outdoor sketches. He bought one of them—the drawing of a fish—for the unheard-of sum of twenty-five dollars. Dan returned to the map company office and told his boss, "Mr. Sanborn, I won't be back for a while. I'm on vacation." He remained "on vacation" for the rest of his life.

To get training for his new profession as an artist, Beard joined the Art Students League. Here he soon became friends with some of the young artists of the day: Charles Dana Gibson and his brother Langdon, Charles and Frederick Lamb, Howard Pyle, Frederic Remington, and others.

Beard started writing about his early outdoor experiences and illustrating his articles with his own drawings. He soon was established as an author-artist through articles in *St. Nicholas* and *Youth's Companion.* A collection of these articles, *American Boys' Handy Book,* was published in 1882 by Charles Scribner's Sons and became very popular among young readers. He followed the success of this book with others covering the same general subjects: *Outdoor Handy Book* and *Jack-of-All-Trades.*

With his ability as an artist established in juvenile magazines, Beard broke into adult publications. An illustration of a Chinese story in *Cosmopolitan* brought Beard to the atten-

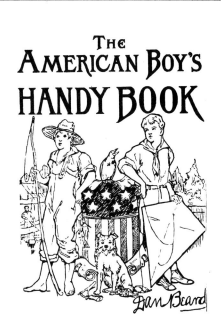

The pen-and-ink sketches that Dan Beard made for his *Handy Books* were simple work drawings. His illustrations for Mark Twain's *A Connecticut Yankee* were in the ornate style of the day, and the one reproduced here was hand-colored by Beard himself.

tion of Mark Twain. Twain picked him to illustrate *A Connecticut Yankee at the Court of King Arthur*. Beard's friendship with Twain lasted until the author's death.

On the basis of his work in promoting outdoor activities for young people, Beard was invited to become the editor of *Recreation*, an influential magazine dedicated to the outdoors. The

Dan Beard was of medium height, with a clipped mustache and neatly trimmed goatee. His favorite costume was an elaborate version of the buckskin outfit he had designed for his Sons of Daniel Boone.

Dan Beard, in his early books, had depicted Daniel Boone and other "American Knights in Buckskin." He made a similar drawing of a boy in buckskin to suggest a costume for his Sons of Daniel Boone to wear.

Norman Rockwell first met Dan Beard, who was an associate editor of *Boys' Life,* in 1914. Sixteen years later, Norman traveled to "Uncle Dan's" home in Suffern, N. Y., to paint him in celebration of his eightieth birthday. Beard wanted to be portrayed in his Daniel Boone outfit but finally agreed to put on a broad-brimmed Scout hat and a Scout neckerchief.
SCOUT MEMORIES 1931

business manager suggested to the new editor that he should establish a department in the magazine of special interest to boy readers. Beard accepted the suggestion. He called his department "The Society of the Sons of Daniel Boone." One of the principal purposes of the "Society" was "to awaken in the boys of today admiration for the old-fashioned virtues of American Knights in Buckskin and a desire to emulate them." In 1909 he collected his ideas into a book that he called *Boy Pioneers and Sons of Daniel Boone.*

Because of his interest in boys' activities, Dan Beard enthusiastically joined in the formation of the Boy Scouts of America. As National Commissioner he influenced the new movement greatly by bringing into it the spirit, the survival skills, and the handicrafts of the American pioneers.

The third man who greatly influenced the formation of the Boy Scouts of America was James E. West, the young Washington lawyer who, on January 1, 1911, became the organization's first Chief Scout Executive. He laid the foundation on which the movement still functions.

Jimmy was born in Washington, D.C., in 1876. Unlike Seton and Beard, he had a tragic, friendless childhood. His father died before he was born. When Jimmy was six, his mother died of tuberculosis. Jimmy was alone, without any known relatives, and was sent to an orphanage.

After his first year there, Jimmy started to limp and complained about pains in one hip. At the hospital it was discovered

300,000 COPIES GUARANTEED CIRCULATION

BOYS' LIFE 10¢

James E. West, the first Chief Scout Executive of the Boy Scouts of America, was a man of great determination and courage. By exerting his forceful personality, he laid the foundation on which the movement still rests. In this 1936 *Boys' Life* cover portrait by Albert A. Rose he is wearing the Silver Buffalo award. The four red and four green service stars represent twenty-four years of work with the Boy Scouts.

that he had a tubercular hip and he was confined to bed.

After Jimmy had spent two years in the hospital, the doctors concluded that he was an incurable cripple and sent him back to the orphanage. He was unable to do the work expected of the boys so was set to the humiliating job of sewing with the girls.

When Jimmy was twelve, one of his mother's old friends, Mrs. Ellis Spear, came to see him. She brought him a children's book she had written and invited him to visit her home and to meet her five children. By continued friendly persuasion, Mrs. Spear interested Jimmy in reading and encouraged him in his determination to get an education.

By the time he graduated from high school Jimmy had made up his mind to become a lawyer. To support himself he worked at the Washington Y.M.C.A. and as a stenographer for the government.

After graduation from law school at twenty-five, West was appointed to the Board of Pension Appeals. Shortly afterwards he took a further step upward, becoming an assistant attorney in the Department of the Interior. Remembering his own childhood, he threw himself into an effort to secure better living conditions for children. He worked to persuade Congress to establish a Children's Court for the District of Columbia. With this accomplished, he looked to the needs of children throughout the country.

With its military-looking coat, breeches, and puttees, the original American Scout uniform *(below)*, designed by members of the Committee on Scout Uniform, Badges, and Awards, was quite different from Baden-Powell's design *(opposite page)*. Within a couple of years it was greatly modified and simplified according to the original concept.

He made a personal appeal to President Theodore Roosevelt and convinced him to call a conference on child care. The eventual outcome of this first White House Conference on the Care of Dependent Children was the establishment of the Children's Bureau of the Department of Labor.

West had become recognized as a social worker of vision, originality and drive—just the kind of person needed to provide a strong impetus to a new movement. He was about to enter a prominent Washington law firm but let himself be persuaded to take on the leadership of the Boy Scouts of America instead.

And so, on January 2, 1911, James E. West opened a national Scout office in the Fifth Avenue Building at 200 Fifth Avenue, New York, with a staff of seven.

The task that confronted West was to form from the dominantly British Boy Scout scheme designed by Baden-Powell an American movement with an American program that would be attractive to American boys.

He appealed to prominent men who had knowledge of youth work and experts in all fields related to Scouting to come to the aid of the Boy Scouts. Formed into committees, they were to accomplish four different tasks. They were to (1) standardize the Scout Oath, the Scout Law and the requirements for Scout advancement, (2) design an American Scout uniform, Scout badges and awards, (3) establish a permanent organizational structure, and (4) develop ways of financing the new movement. The committees accomplished their objectives in four months. The foundation was laid for a strong national movement.

Meanwhile, the work of creating an American Boy Scout manual was proceeding. A preliminary *Official Handbook* had been put together the year before by combining the main features of Baden-Powell's *Scouting for Boys* with some of Seton's *Birch-Bark Roll* material. Now West, working with an editorial board, secured the help of outstanding specialists in writing chapters on their areas of expertise for a new book. Camping and bird study, first aid and conservation, mapping and signaling, Indian lore and pioneer skills, citizenship and patriotism, and many other subjects were covered. As soon as the new Scout Oath and Law, the new Scout requirements, and the uniform and badge designs were approved, the book went to press. The first edition of this *Handbook for Boys* came out on August 31, 1911.

With the organization firmly established and the guidelines set, the Boy Scouts of America was launched on its course of involving the boys of America in the adventure of Scouting.

From the very beginning, West and the members of the executive board realized that the growing movement would need some kind of publication that would reach the boys directly to help them in their Scout work and that would inform boys and leaders alike about what was happening in Scouting around the country. A committee was appointed early in 1912 to consider the matter.

The committee soon learned that a young man of eighteen, Joseph Lane, was already publishing a Scout magazine in Providence, Rhode Island. He had presumed, with youthful innocence, to call it "the semiofficial publication of the Boy Scouts of America, and the official organ of the Rhode Island Boy Scouts." He had hit upon the perfect title for a boys' magazine: *Boys' Life.* After considerable negotiation, Lane and his associates agreed to sell their publication for a sum equal to one dollar for every bona-fide subscription. There were 6,100 subscriptions. This fixed the price at $6,100. The Boy Scouts of America embarked on its magazine-publishing enterprise with the July 1912 issue of *Boys' Life.*

The first editor was Edward Cave, a former sports reporter and at the time the editor of *Recreation.* Cave knew his Scouting. He was the Scoutmaster of an active Mamaroneck, New York, troop and had written numerous articles on Scouting subjects. He immediately set out to turn the magazine into a major national youth publication.

The first issue of *Boys' Life,* which appeared on March 1, 1911, was a very creditable production of forty-eight pages, put out by an eighteen-year-old Rhode Island boy. Several of its stories were taken from *The Scout,* the weekly British Scout magazine founded by Baden-Powell.

Norman Rockwell and Boys' Life Magazine

During his 1913–16 period with *Boys' Life,* Norman worked as an illustrator and as an art director. He created eleven cover paintings and more than two hundred illustrations for stories and articles. After 1916 he continued to do an occasional *Boys' Life* cover, such as this one which was also used as a poster promoting the first National Jamboree in Washington, D.C., in 1935.

Norman Rockwell hit *Boys' Life* at exactly the right time.

When the ambitious eighteen-year-old artist walked into the *Boys' Life* office on that fall day in 1912, Edward Cave, the editor, had just finished writing an editorial for the December issue promising his readers great things for 1913. The page size of the magazine would be increased to the size of the *Saturday Evening Post* and the *Literary Digest,* the style-setters of American magazines in those days. The authors would be outstanding, the illustrations would be tops. Cave had selected the stories he intended to run in the early issues of the coming year, but had only started to line up the artists.

But he had other things on his mind as well. In addition to his task of editing *Boys' Life,* Cave had been busy finishing the manuscript for a boys' book on hiking and overnight camping for Doubleday, Page and Company—the same house that had published Ernest Thompson Seton's early attempt at an official handbook for the Boy Scouts of America. He needed an illustrator for his book.

Cave greeted Norman warmly. He was impressed with the work that Norman pulled out of his portfolio. He recognized the young artist's potential. But Cave was also deeply aware that

the budget for *Boys' Life* was pinched. He had to secure art work at the lowest possible rates. A young, beginning artist with sufficient skill to satisfy the magazine's readers would fit his requirements nicely.

Cave decided to give Norman a *Boys' Life* story to illustrate. He also asked him to try his hand at illustrating his hiking book. Norman admitted that he was not much of an outdoorsman. No matter. Cave's main need was for a few full-page illustrations and a suitable heading for each chapter. When it came to technical drawings, he would give Norman all the necessary details.

Norman went home to the New York boardinghouse where he lived with his parents and older brother and got to work.

If it hadn't been for Thomas Fogarty, Norman might never have joined the Boy Scouts. It was Fogarty, Norman's teacher in the illustration class of the Art Students League, who had sent the young Rockwell to the office of the *Boys' Life* editor.

Fogarty, at that stage, was just the right art teacher for Norman.

Norman had already been exposed to the academic approach to art. While still a schoolboy, he had studied at the Chase School of Art in New York City. After leaving school at the age of sixteen, he had signed up at the National Academy of Art and had learned to draw the human body from plaster casts of antique sculptures and from stiffly-posed life-class models. Within a couple of months he had tired of the Academy's stiff and academic sessions. He had switched to the League, where he had enrolled in the life classes of George B. Bridgman. Under this eminent teacher, he had reached the point where he could sit down and draw the human figure offhand, at rest or in vigorous action, by constructing it from the bones and muscle masses with which Bridgman had made him so intimately acquainted.

But his training, so far, had been in fine art. And Norman was not particularly interested in fine art. He wanted to become

an illustrator. For this pursuit, he joined the classes of Thomas Fogarty at the League.

Fogarty was a noted illustrator whose work appeared regularly in magazines and books. He would have someone in his class read a story from a current magazine or would tell a story himself. He would then have his pupils suggest what scene in the story they would pick to illustrate and how they would go about developing the illustration. He insisted on complete faithfulness to the author's intentions. "An illustration," he would say, " is an illustration. Nothing less, nothing more. A meeting of artist and author. An author's words in paint, gentlemen and ladies, an author's words in paint." He also insisted on authenticity. If the author had a character sitting in a Windsor chair, the illustration must show the character sitting in a Windsor chair, and in no other kind of chair—even if the illustrator had to go to the Metropolitan Museum of Art to see what a Windsor chair looked like. Norman absorbed and accepted each of his teacher's dicta—his emphasis on authenticity was often carried almost to the point of fanaticism.

Fogarty had a special incentive for encouraging his pupils to do their best: From time to time, when a publisher wanted him to illustrate a book or story and caught him overloaded with commitments, he would use the publisher's request as a challenge to his pupils, turning the commission into a class assignment. If a member of the class handed in an acceptable illustration, he would be paid for it and would see his work in print.

In 1911 when the American Book Company was planning a book about Samuel de Champlain, the sixteenth-century French explorer who founded Quebec, Fogarty was asked to do a frontispiece. He was too busy at the time, so assigned the task to his class. Norman came out the winner and, at the age of seventeen, saw the publication of his first book illustration. "I had a terrible time with it," he recalled later. "I didn't know enough about perspective to show the river lower than the parapet on which Champlain stands."

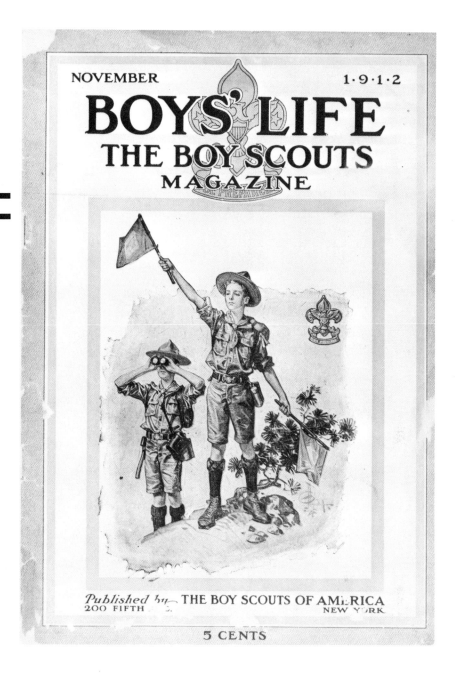

NOVEMBER 1·9·1·2

BOYS' LIFE
THE BOY SCOUTS
MAGAZINE

Published by THE BOY SCOUTS OF AMERICA
200 FIFTH AV. NEW YORK

5 CENTS

J. C. Leyendecker's painting on the November 1912 issue of *Boys' Life* was originally a *Saturday Evening Post* cover presented to the Boy Scouts by the editor of the *Post*. It next became the cover of the official *Handbook for Boys*. It took a year for someone to notice that the Leyendecker Scout was using Morse code signal flags for sending a nonexisting semaphore letter. Norman did not make these mistakes when he made his signaling painting *(left)* for *The Red Cross Magazine:* the flags are semaphore flags and the letter is the *L* of the semaphore alphabet.

Soon after, when Robert McBride & Company needed illustrations for a new volume in Carl Harry Caludy's popular *Tell Me Why* series of children's books, Fogarty sent Norman down to the publisher with his portfolio. Result: he did a dozen illustrations and was paid the princely sum of a hundred and fifty dollars.

Something similar happened in the fall of 1912. Fogarty learned that the Boy Scouts of America, established only two years before, had bought the rights to a minor New England boys' magazine and was planning to turn it into a major national magazine for boys. Fogarty had seen an advance copy of the November issue that had a cover painting by Joseph C. Leyendecker, one of the country's leading artists and one of his and Norman's favorite illustrators.

Pen and ink drawings from the *Boy Scout's Hike Book*.

He called in his star pupil. "Norman," he said, "the Boy Scouts are publishing a magazine they call *Boys' Life*. Why don't you go down to their national office and see if they have some work for you?"

Norman did. They had.

In illustrating his story for the January 1913 *Boys' Life,* Norman followed the procedure that Fogarty had taught him.

He read the manuscript a couple of times before beginning work on the illustrations. It was a story by Stanley Snow, a popular writer of boys' fiction. The locale was "the wilderness of British America," a Canadian lumber area. The plot involved three characters: "a raw English boy of eighteen, ex-waif of the streets of London," a rough "lumber boss," and a Cree Indian. It started with a brawl in a company store, then continued with a twenty-two-mile snowshoe trek through the winter bleakness of the Canadian brush. It wound up with a revenge attack by the Indian, who had discovered that the lumber boss had emptied his beaver traps.

For his first *Boys' Life* assignment, Norman made three charcoal drawings for Stanley Snow's story "Partners"—a two-man fight in the snow, a snowshoe trek, and an episode in which the cheated Indian almost kills the hero, who has been tricked by the villain into exchanging coats with him. The snow below and the blank sky above did not give Norman much opportunity to render background, or to model his figures. But the editor liked the drawings well enough to give Norman three other assignments.

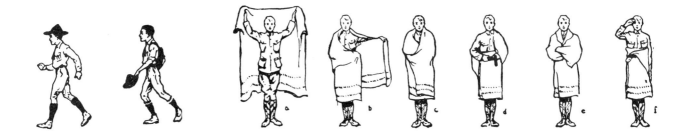

Norman's illustrations satisfied Cave. He accepted them and gave Norman three other stories to illustrate—a Western, a baseball story, and a track story.

Norman's pen-and-ink drawings for Cave's hiking book were progressing with extraordinary speed. By mid-winter, when Norman finished the job, he had produced 106 illustrations. When the book appeared in the spring of 1913 under the title *The Boy Scout's Hike Book,* it was accepted as the best-illustrated and best-written book on the market on the subjects of hiking and overnight camping.

Norman's art work pleased Cave, and he offered him the job of being *Boys' Life*'s regular artist at a monthly salary of fifty dollars. For this amount he was to produce a cover and the illustrations for a story each month. Norman accepted, with the proviso that he be permitted to do art work for other magazines and book publishers, as long as this did not interfere with his

Among the drawings that Norman made for Cave's *Boy Scout's Hike Book*, the full-page illustrations and the chapter headings are particularly interesting as examples of the skill he had developed in using pen and ink.

Boys' Life responsibilities. Cave agreed. And Norman was established in the office, with his own chair, desk, and easel.

In June 1913, *Boys' Life* had been the property of the Boy Scouts of America for one full year. It had made great strides. It had more than doubled its subscription list. It had been turned into a modern-looking magazine. Financially it had lived up to its promise to pay for itself. As a matter of fact, it ended its first year with a surplus—of $1.76.

But at the end of this first year, an editorial upheaval took place in the magazine. Edward Cave and *Boys' Life* came to a parting of the ways. W. P. McGuire, formerly a reporter on the *New York Sun* and the *New York Times,* and more recently assistant Sunday editor for the *St. Paul Pioneer Press and Dispatch,* became the editor with the September issue of the magazine.

While this was going on Norman was wondering what it might mean to him, whether he might suddenly find himself out of the job he had so recently accepted. He discovered that he had nothing to worry about. McGuire had looked at his work and had found it completely acceptable. As a matter of fact, he suggested that Norman take on more work than he had been doing. The magazine would pay him for the extra illustrations he made, beyond his regular monthly salary for his regular work.

And so, for the next year, starting with the September 1913 issue, Norman produced a cover for each issue—except for a

Most of Norman's *Boys' Life* illustrations were done in charcoal. But he occasionally worked in oil. During his *Boys' Life* period he had a chance to depict a great variety of activities, from canoeing on quiet

lakes to horseback-riding across wide prairies. For a while he was enamored of galloping horses. He drew them being ridden by Indians and cowboys, by Union and Confederate soldiers.

PRESIDENT WILSON'S MESSAGE TO 9,000,000 SCHOOL BOYS

BOYS' LIFE

THE BOY SCOUTS' MAGAZINE

"Waves of the Moon"
By John Fleming Wilson

September, 1913

PUBLISHED BY THE BOY SCOUTS OF AMERICA

Norman's first cover picture, on the September 1913 *Boys' Life*, introduced Patrol Leader Tad Shelton, the hero of several John Fleming Wilson stories the artist was to illustrate. The stories told of the adventures of Tad and his patrol along the Oregon coast—a smuggling plot, a mysterious shipwreck, steering a disabled ship into safe harbor, rescuing sailors on a life raft.

couple of months when McGuire decided to use a photographic cover. In addition, he illustrated two or three stories for each issue, running up a total for the year of 101 oil paintings, charcoals, and pen-and-ink vignettes. He illustrated everything that came his way: stories of Indians and pioneers, hunters and cowboys, stories about baseball and football, sailing and canoeing, about boys becoming First Class Scouts and young men getting up in life Horatio Alger-style.

Most of the early covers that Norman painted for *Boys' Life* followed the popular style of the *Saturday Evening Post*. They featured a single character engaged in some action against a plain background. Occasionally he went all out, filling the entire cover with an exciting painting depicting the climax of one of the stories in the magazine.

A thrilling serial, "The Trail to the El Dorado," gave Norman full opportunity to use his artistic imagination. It dealt with two boys' adventures in a dangerous pre-Civil War journey across plains and mountains, and involved cowboys and Indians.

left: In 1913, Norman broke into *Youth's Companion,* and soon after sold illustrations to *American Boy* and *Everyland.* The editor of *St. Nicholas* gave him several Ralph Henry Barbour stories to illustrate. Two of the characters and one of the incidents in "The Magic Football" are pictured here

below: The pen-and-ink sketches for *The Boy's Camp Book,* drawn by the nineteen-year-old Rockwell, are noteworthy for their composition and details. Most of the instructional drawings in the book feature the heavy camp equipment that was popular before World War I.

With a portfolio bulging with published art, Norman set out to conquer the other magazines in the juvenile field. It was not long before all the major juvenile magazines were assigning stories and articles to him. Shortly, several book publishers asked him to illustrate their books. One of them was Cave's publisher. Cave had written another book for boys, this one about camping. Norman drew fifty-seven pen-and-ink drawings for it. It appeared in 1914 under the name of *The Boy's Camp Book.*

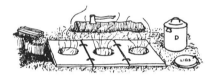

In working for *Boys' Life,* Norman took particular pains with his sports illustrations. He knew that his young readers would recognize and complain about any mistake he made in depicting the positions and actions of sportsmen—particularly those of his baseball and football players.

As he was growing up, Norman had been a skinny kid—not unhealthy but without the strength and inclination to take part in sports and other vigorous activities in which other kids indulged. His older brother, Jarvis, was the athlete in the family. Norman was just "a lump, a long skinny nothing, a bean pole without the beans."

Norman's sketches illustrating baseball stories add up to an almost complete stop-motion series of all the positions of pitching and batting, running and sliding. He tried to instill the same vigor into his drawings of boys playing football, basketball, and hockey, and into a dramatic story illustration of an underwater swimming rescue.

Norman's frail physique had been a concern to him. "Boys who are athletes are expressing themselves fully," he wrote later. "They have an identity, a recognized place among the other boys. I didn't have that. All I had was the ability to draw, which as far as I could see didn't count for much. But because it was all I had, I began to make it my whole life. I drew all the time. Gradually my narrow shoulders, long neck, and pigeon toes became less important to me. My feelings no longer paralyzed me. I drew and drew and drew."

And that was why Norman, at the age of thirteen, had decided that the life of an artist was the life for him.

Now, when he had to illustrate stories of baseball and football and other sports he turned to Jarvis for help. Jarvis assumed any position a story called for and modeled patiently while Norman sketched him. Before long, Norman was so famil-

A 1914 illustration for a sea story, "The Boys Aboard the *Vanguard*," has some of the photographic qualities that Norman was to perfect later in his career.

The ultramodern racing cars that Norman depicted in 1915 are the antiques of today. An expert on old cars might be able to recognize the five models speeding across these pages.

iar with all the details of the various poses that he was able to release his brother from his modeling chores.

In all probability, it was Norman's father, J. Waring Rockwell, who had initiated him into art by encouraging his early scribblings.

The elder Rockwell was the manager of the New York office of the Philadelphia cotton-goods firm of George Wood, Sons, & Company. He liked to draw. He spent many spare-time

hours copying illustrations from magazines and books, but rarely produced anything original. Norman was different. He was not very old before he began to use his imagination in sketching houses and ships, animals and trees, pirates and Indians, incidents from books he read. But his greatest incentive was his father's readings.

In the evenings, after Norman and Jarvis had finished their homework, the family would gather around the dining-room table. The elder Rockwell would bring out one of the works of a favorite author, Charles Dickens, and read it aloud by the light of a gas lamp. Mrs. Rockwell would be sewing. Jarvis might be fiddling, but Norman would be busy drawing Dickens' characters: Mr. Pickwick and Uriah Heep, Oliver Twist and Mr. Micawber, Fagin and Bill Sikes, Bob Cratchit and Tiny Tim. Whenever his father read the description of one of the characters, Norman would ask him to repeat the details so that he would get them right; so that Mr. Micawber's tall hat and Fagin's swirling cloak would look the way they should. His

From the beginning of his career, Norman experimented with a special signature. He eventually developed a whole string of them: a smooth, Spencerian, handwritten *norman rockwell,* or, occasionally, NORMAN ROCKWELL, and finally the hollow-letter style he invented for himself.

Norman tried to incorporate his initials into a monogram: "Print a capital *N*. On the first vertical of this *N*, draw the loop of a *P* so that it touches the second vertical of the *N*. From this, in turn, draw the loop and slanting line of an *R*." The monogram *(below)* was as complicated and as unintelligible as his description of it. He soon abandoned it.

favorite Dickens characters were to become important figures in many of his future paintings.

Norman's mother, the daughter of an English-born artist, Howard Hill, took a proprietory interest in her son's art. Proud of her English ancestry, Nancy Hill Rockwell had insisted on naming her second son for a supposed forebear, a Sir Norman Percevel, who, reputedly, kicked Guy Fawkes of Gunpowder Plot fame down the stairs of the Tower of London. "Remember, Norman," she would say, again and again, "it is spelled with an *e*—*i* and *a* are common." When he learned to write, she made sure that he always signed his name "Norman Percevel Rockwell." Now that he began to have his art published, she insisted that each drawing and painting carry this full name.

Norman obeyed. Although he disliked the name Percevel, the complete name appeared on most of his *Boys' Life* illustrations. Sometimes he abbreviated it to "Norman P. Rockwell." His credit line, however, was always "Illustrations by Norman Percevel Rockwell."

When it came time for Norman to paint the cover for the

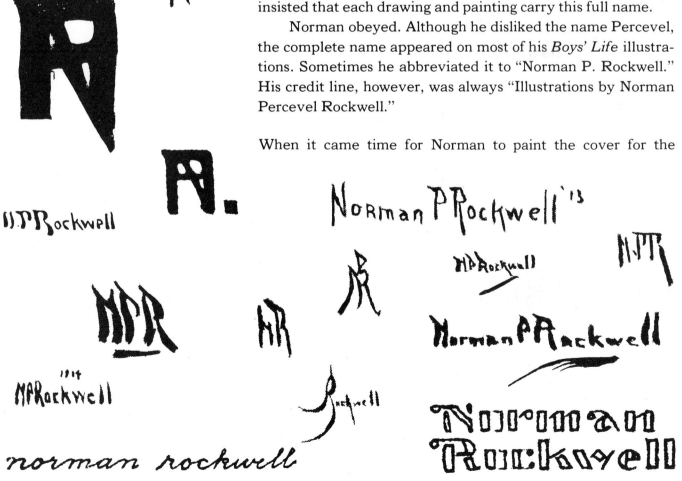

EX-PRESIDENT ROOSEVELT— TO ALL BOYS

BOYS' LIFE

THE BOY SCOUTS' MAGAZINE

10 Cts.

Read
The Story Without a Title
($10.00 Cash Prize for Title)

Also the
Extraordinary Announcement
Pages 2 and 3

December
1913

PUBLISHED BY THE BOY SCOUTS OF AMERICA

Norman P Rockwell

December 1913 issue of *Boys' Life,* he decided to give all the Boy Scouts of the United States a special "Christmas card" in the form of a combined Boy Scout-Santa Claus painting. He had a sentimental reason for doing this: the first art "commission" he had ever had was for a series of Christmas cards.

It happened in 1909 when he was still in school and was trying to earn money for his art classes. He bought a special kind of "mail route" from another boy. It ran from the town of Mamaroneck, New York, where the Rockwell family was living at the time, out to fashionable Orienta Point, where there were large estates.

Every morning at half-past five Norman collected the mail at the post office and bicycled the two and a half miles to the tip of the point, stopping along the way to deliver each customer's mail. Within a week he was making $2.50 a day.

One of his customers was Mrs. James Constable, the widow of one of the owners of Arnold Constable, a New York department store. She found out about Norman's desire to become an artist and asked him regularly how he was getting along.

When Christmas came around, Mrs. Constable told him that she had a job for him. Each year she was accustomed to sending out specially printed greetings to her many relatives. Was Norman interested in drawing four original Christmas cards for her? He was and did. "She paid me very well," he remembered many years later. "Outrageously, in fact, considering my inexperience."

The cover of the December 1913 *Boys' Life* was the first of many "Boy Scout-Good Turn" paintings and numerous Christmas covers, several of them involving Santa Claus, that Rockwell would do over the years. In this particular instance, he never revealed how Santa managed to get himself thrown out of his sky-roaming reindeer sleigh to land in such an ignominious predicament.

In 1915 the Rockwell family made another of the many moves it had made periodically since Norman was born in New York City on February 3, 1894. This time the move was to the suburb of New Rochelle. Norman was happy about his new home. In New Rochelle it was easy to get models for his paintings. He rounded up the kind of boy types he wanted, and they posed for him for fifty cents an hour.

They were a restless lot of youngsters, hard to keep still long enough for Norman to catch their poses. They agreed to twenty-five-minute sessions, followed by five-minute breaks, but often got fidgety before the time was up. Norman invented a remedy. At the beginning of each modeling session he placed a stack of five nickels on a table beside his easel. Every twenty-five minutes, when it was time for the break, he moved the stack of nickels to the other side of the table. "Now, that's your pile," he would inform his model. He had no further problems.

In New Rochelle, Norman located three of the best boy models he ever had. One of them, Billy Paine, was especially outstanding. Billy had the born actor's ability to assume any pose and facial expression. Norman used him in countless illustrations and on the covers of *Boys' Life*.

Up to this time Norman had been his own art director for his own work for *Boys' Life* and had been the magazine's only artist. He had assigned stories to himself to illustrate and had approved his own artwork. Now, with numerous outside commitments and having to commute to New York from New Rochelle, he found it harder and harder to produce for *Boys' Life* all the illustrations the editor wanted.

W. P. McGuire agreed that Norman could try to attract other artists to do the *Boys' Life* covers and some of the illustrations. He would illustrate whatever he could manage, concentrating mostly on serials. In addition he would do the job of a regular art director: he would come into the office once a week to interview artists, assign stories, and approve the finished art. His monthly salary would be raised to seventy-five dollars.

Norman quickly put to work some of the especially gifted artists studying at the Art Students League and secured a variety of other illustrators. He himself was working on the illustrations for three serials simultaneously: *The Story of Daniel Boone* by Everett T. Tomlinson, William Heyliger's *Don Strong of the Wolf Patrol,* and Walter Walden's *The Moonshiners in the Jungle*. The illustrations were the best he had ever done for *Boys' Life*.

The Illustrator at Work
" N. P. R."—Mr. Norman P. Rockwell, who is painting the pictures for Mr. Tomlinson's great story, "snapped" at his easel in his studio.

DANIEL BOONE AT THE
AGE 85.

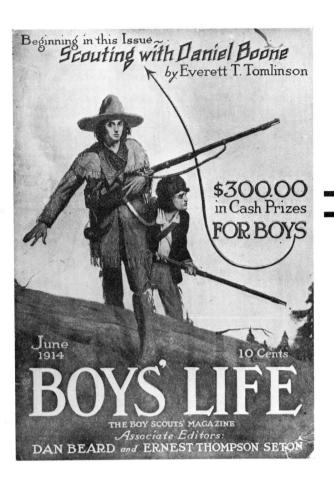

In 1914, *Boys' Life* ran a serial, "Scouting with Daniel Boone," by Everett T. Tomlinson, the author of some twenty noted historical books for boys. The editor expressed the hope that "reading this account will quicken the interest of boys in the early history of our country and increase their admiration for the good qualities which, under trying circumstances, distinguished men like Boone." Norman was featured as the artist and took great pains with the illustrations.

Boys' Life sponsored a contest in connection with Tomlinson's serial. After finishing the story, the reader was to submit an essay describing "the qualities of Daniel Boone which made him a good Scout and a valuable citizen, and why those qualities are important in life today." First prize was $50.00, second prize $25.00—attractive sums in 1914.

Walter Walden's highly dramatic serial "The Moonshiners in the Jungle" featured Nat, the narrator and hero; his Uncle Billy; Bat, one of the "moonshiners"; and Joseph DeLong, the revenue officer.

BOYS' LIFE
THE BOY SCOUTS' MAGAZINE

1915
MAY
10 Cents

"Don"

The Hero of William Heyliger's
Great Scout Serial Story In This Issue

He also got busy on two covers. One was an opener for the Don Strong series, of a Scout just sitting there, representing Patrol Leader Don Strong. The other was a picture of a boy diving, one of the earliest examples of the humor and originality that were to make Rockwell famous.

BOYS' LIFE
THE BOY SCOUTS' MAGAZINE

AUGUST
10 CENTS

Norman P Rockwell

Stirring Stories by *Heyliger, Crump, Walden, Elderdice, Rouse, The Cave Scout and Dan Beard*

left: In "Don Strong," Heyliger's patrol leader hero takes off for a strenuous hike, loses his way, climbs a tree to orient himself (and what a tree Norman gave him to climb!), and finally returns home triumphantly.

right: For the August 1915 *Boys' Life* cover Norman painted a boy diving into the water. He had no place to go where he could sketch a dive—no lake or swimming pool. So he simply put his favorite model, Bill Paine, into red-and-white-striped trunks and had him stand on his head while he sketched the boy's wiggling legs, then cut Bill off at the waist and painted a big splash.

Norman's growth as an artist during this period was astonishing. His human figures came alive, his compositions became more imaginative, his ideas more clearly expressed, his techniques more perfected, his details more exact—almost photographic.

This depiction of numerous intricate details became a Rockwell characteristic. The artist believes that he inherited the trait from his maternal grandfather, Howard Hill.

Hill had emigrated to America sometime after the Civil War. He had hoped to make a fortune in his new country as a portrait painter. Instead he fathered twelve children and be-

For a Scout play in the October 1915 *Boys' Life* Norman sketched each of the characters: "The Scout," "The Farmer," "The Tough." For authenticity, he went to locations where he could sketch details mentioned in a story, such as the lunch-room equipment in the January 1915 story about "Pancake Jim."

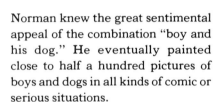

Norman knew the great sentimental appeal of the combination "boy and his dog." He eventually painted close to half a hundred pictures of boys and dogs in all kinds of comic or serious situations.

came a painter of landscapes, animals, and houses. Some of his landscapes were good but brought in only enough to keep the family afloat. The models for his animal paintings were family pets or family prides—large and small dogs, horses, and prize pigs. "He painted in great detail," Norman recalled. "Every hair on the dog was carefully drawn. The tiny highlights in the pig's eyes—great, watery, human eyes—could be clearly seen." The hair and eyes of the dogs that Norman painted have the same details. He is not known ever to have painted a pig.

There can be little doubt that Norman's progress during the years he was connected with *Boys' Life* was brought about by his absolute determination to succeed as an illustrator, the demanding schedule he had set for himself, and his mental attitude. From the very beginning, the Boy Scouts had expected this young, talented artist to do his very best. Now it was Norman who expected top performance of himself. He expressed it some time later when he painted the figure "100%" in gold paint on his easel. "What does that mean?" a friend asked him. "That's what Norman expects of Norman," he answered.

Norman kept Billy Paine pretty busy—he posed for all three boys on the first Rockwell *Saturday Evening Post* cover *(right)* and for both circus characters on a later one. The next year Norman's sophisticated young man and woman made the *Post* and the artist had the last laugh on his friend who had ridiculed the picture.

Norman was getting along all right. He was prospering. But he was beginning to dream of getting into the big money, getting his work accepted by major adult magazines, even getting himself on the cover of that day's dominant magazine, the prestigious *Saturday Evening Post*.

He began working up sophisticated ideas: a party-dressed girl entertained by a collar-ad swain, a spotlighted ballerina curtseying before her audience. He showed his sketches to his friend and studio mate, Clyde Forsythe.

Clyde smirked. Awful! Hopeless! The *Post* would never accept anything as trite as that. He snatched up a sketch that Norman had been working on for a possible *Boys' Life* cover. "Do what you know how to do: kids. Do something like this— just do a more finished job to match the quality the *Post* expects of its cover artists."

Norman was dubious. Nevertheless, he went to work on a different idea. He sketched a boy dressed in his Sunday best pushing a baby carriage, with a couple of boys in baseball uniforms jeering at him. He called in his favorite model, Billy Paine, and had him pose for all three boys.

Then another painting: a boy circus barker in a top hat presenting the "strong man," dressed in long underwear, to an

THE SATURDAY EVENING POST

FRANCE AND THE NEW AGE—By Will Irwi

THE SATURDAY EVENING POST

An Illustrated Weekly
Founded A... ...8 by Benj. Franklin

MAY 20, 1916   5c. THE COPY

Norman
Rockwell

THE EMPIRE BUILDERS—By Mary Roberts Rinehart

audience of boys and girls, again with Bill as model for both main characters. Finally: rough sketches for three more cover ideas.

Norman packed up his finished art in a large, unwieldly, oilcloth-covered carrying case that a harness maker had made for him. On a cold March morning in 1916 he took the train for Philadelphia and marched into the *Saturday Evening Post* office. His entry reminded him of the time three and a half years before when he had stepped into the national office of the Boy Scouts of America.

"May I help you?" asked the receptionist.

"I should like to see the editor."

"You are an artist?"

"Yes."

"It is the art editor you want to see, then."

The receptionist picked up the telephone. After a short conversation, she turned to Norman.

"Mr. Dower will be out to see you."

In a little while Norman found himself face to face with Walter H. Dower, the highly respected art editor of the *Post*. He opened his large portfolio case and brought out his two finished paintings and his sketches. Dower looked at them, then picked them up and carried them into another office.

While waiting in the anteroom, Norman studied the original oils by famous *Post* artists hanging on the walls: Leyendecker, Howard Chandler Christy, Coles Phillips, James Montgomery Flagg, Maxfield Parrish, N. C. Wyeth. He marveled at his own audacity in believing that he could match himself against such greats.

The wait seemed eternal. Finally Dower reappeared. There was a smile on his face.

"I have conferred with Mr. Lorimer, our editor. We'll take

Norman's love affair with the *Saturday Evening Post* started in 1916 and lasted for forty-seven years. During this period he painted 319 covers and a great number of story illustrations.

both of your paintings. And we would like you to do three more covers along the lines of your sketches." He wound up the interview by placing an envelope in the hand of the speechless young artist and wishing him luck.

As soon as Norman was outside the office door he opened the envelope. He took out its contents: a check for seventy-five dollars.

He was elated. A cover on the *Post!* Two covers on the *Post!!* An audience of two million! Seventy-five dollars for one painting! He had arrived!

Norman's last piece of artwork for the Boy Scouts—for the time being—appeared in the *Boys' Life* issue for March 1916, the same month in which his cover illustrations were accepted by the *Saturday Evening Post.*

The first stage of Norman's career had ended. His apprenticeship was over. He said good-bye to the first and only salaried job he ever held. He was completely on his own—a free-lance artist ready to conquer the world with his art.

And there was a large field to be conquered. The war in Europe was in its second year. The United States had entered upon a period of military "preparedness" for war. Business was booming. Magazines were prospering.

Sentiment for war against Germany burst into flame on March 18, 1917, when three unarmed American merchantmen were sunk without warning by German U-boats.

President Woodrow Wilson appeared before Congress on April 2, 1917. "The world must be made safe for democracy," he said. The Senate and the House passed the declaration of war against Germany, and the president signed it on April 6. America was at war.

Within days, Congress adopted selective conscription.

When Norman appeared before his draft board he was classified "Exempt." He was not told why. He felt guilty about not joining the war effort. He wanted to do his part, and his first attempt was through his art. He painted a couple of covers for the *Post,* both of them reflecting his continued interest in the Boy Scouts. The first (May 12, 1917) showed a Scout at smart salute, as the flag passed by. Behind him, raising his hat, was an old veteran from a previous war. The other (June 16, 1917) was a humorous picture of a Scout, decked out in all his finery, measuring an undersized boy standing next to a crude MEN WANTED sign.

But painting patriotic magazine covers was not enough. Norman wanted the real thing. And so, one day in June 1917, he took a train to New York City and entered the Navy enlistment center at City Hall. He was turned down by the recruiting yeoman—he was seventeen pounds underweight for his height and age. But . . . "Let's go see the doctor."

What happened then is best told in Norman's own words:

"'Norm's an artist,' said the recruiting officer. 'If we get him in they'll give him a special assignment, painting the insignia on airplane wings or something. It won't matter if he's underweight.'

"'How much under is he?' said the doctor.

"'Seventeen pounds,' said the yeoman.

"'Won't do,' said the doctor. 'We can waive ten pounds, but not seventeen.'

"'How about the treatment?' asked the yeoman.

"'I want to get in. What's the treatment?'

"'Bananas, doughnuts, and water. You eat seven pounds' worth, we waive the other ten pounds, and you're in.'

"I began to eat doughnuts and bananas and drink the water. 'I'm going to burst!' I stuffed . . . and stuffed . . . and stuffed.

"The yeoman weighed me again. 'Hurrah!' he shouted. 'We've won!' And the doctor and he congratulated each other. I could hardly walk."

A few days later, Norman was called to duty as a "landsman for quartermaster"—a sailor of little experience assigned to special duties. Norman's duties would be those of a painter and varnisher.

In spite of Norman's efforts to see action, he wound up in

During his Navy hitch, Norman occasionally added to the signature on his paintings his naval designation of U.S.N.R.F.

THE SATURDAY EVENING POST

MAY 12, 1917

WHAT OF THE EAST—By SAMUEL G. BLYTHE
THE SUB-DEB—By MARY ROBERTS RINEHART

THE SATURDAY EVENING POST

JUNE 16, 1917

In This Number: Carl W. Ackerman—Maximilian Foster—Will Irwin—Basil King
Charles E. Van Loan—Elizabeth Jordan—Nalbro Bartley—Eleanor Franklin Egan

Charleston, South Carolina. "Your job is morale," he was told. His navy career became a sinecure. Two days a week he was required to make layouts and draw cartoons for *Afloat and Ashore,* the camp newspaper. The other days, on his own initiative, he drew and painted portraits of officers and ordinary sailors, as part of his "morale" work. Beyond that he was allowed to pursue his own career and to take on any outside art assignment.

During his navy days—June 1917 to November 1918—he did five covers for the *Post,* two for *Life,* a couple for *Country Gentleman,* and a few commercial jobs. An ensign friend of his figured out that with his earnings and free room and board and clothing provided by the Navy he was making more than his admiral.

He also got himself involved in a few special assignments.

James Montgomery Flagg had produced for the war effort his famous "I want YOU !" poster, showing Uncle Sam pointing his finger directly at the onlooker. J. C. Leyendecker had made a spectacular painting for the *Post* to back the Government's Liberty Loan drive: it was entitled *Weapons for Liberty* and depicted a Boy Scout, kneeling on one knee, presenting a sword emblazoned with the legend "Be Prepared" to a dramatic and determined young woman representing Liberty. The *Post* had turned the painting into a poster for distribution and display throughout the country. Now Norman painted a poster for the Boy Scouts to promote some of the other war service projects they were undertaking.

Leyendecker's *Weapons for Liberty* poster *(left)* and Rockwell's Boy Scout "war service" poster *(below)*.

The four pictures with Scout subjects that Norman painted for *The Red Cross Magazine* in 1918—among them the campfire on the opposite page—were his first efforts at using all the colors of his palette. Up to that time his *Boys' Life* and *Post* covers had been painted in black and red for two-color reproduction.

But Norman had a further commitment. He had accepted a commission from the American National Red Cross for four illustrations for the organization's monthly magazine. Each cover was to have a Boy Scout theme. Norman approached the task with a special enthusiasm and dedication and turned out the finest paintings he had yet done. One showed a Boy Scout signaling with flags from a tall tower, another a Scoutmaster telling a campfire story to his boys. The remaining two dealt with the Daily Good Turn to which every Scout pledges himself. In one, a Scout is depicted helping an elderly man across a crowded city street; in the other, a Scout is bandaging the leg of a tiny puppy.

One of the four was destined to set in motion a project that would be of special significance to Norman and the Boy Scouts of America for more than fifty years to come.

And why should the American National Red Cross have wanted to honor the Boy Scouts by dedicating four pages of its monthly

magazine for November 1918 to the activities and ideals of the movement? For the simple reason that the Red Cross and the Boy Scouts of America were the two largest non-government volunteer service groups in the country, and they had decided to coordinate their activities to increase their effectiveness in the war effort.

The Boy Scouts of America had been growing at a rapid pace during the seven years of its existence. Since its first year, it had more than quintupled its membership and was, at the outbreak of the war, the nation's largest uniformed body, with more than 300,000 members. The Boy Scouts had more than twice the numerical strength of the standing army of the United States, nearly twice that of the National Guard, four times the numerical strength of the United States Navy and eleven times that of the United States Marine Corps. Each Scout was trained for service. His place was at home or near it. His function was to do a boy's work under the guidance of an adult. He was available for immediate mobilization on the home front.

The Scouts were committed to three specific undertakings:

"To cooperate with the Department of Agriculture and Council of National Defense in the extension and development of home gardens, under the slogan 'Every Scout to Feed a Soldier.'

"To cooperate with the Navy Department in organizing an Emergency Coast Patrol along the sea-coast towns.

"To cooperate with the American National Red Cross through its local chapters in meeting their responsibilities occasioned by the state of war."

The Boy Scouts and their leaders leapt into action throughout the country.

During the summer of 1917, Scouts planted thousands of war gardens. The result was that "every Scout" managed to feed not just "a" soldier, but two or three at least.

Along the Atlantic coast, older Scouts helped the Naval authorities maintain a lookout at lighthouses and special sta-

Norman included a chubby Boy Scout with an improvised steel helmet in his February 22, 1919, *Post* cover featuring a well-decorated American soldier returning victoriously from France after World War I.

tions. They acted as messengers and orderlies and sent and received messages by signal flag during the day and with a light at night, flashing the Morse Code they had learned as Scouts.

Because of their first-aid training and life-saving experience it was particularly appropriate that the Boy Scouts should work with the Red Cross. They helped the organization in its financial campaigns. They distributed notices and carried messages on bicycles, motorcycles, or horseback when possible and on foot when there was no other way. They helped obtain, prepare, and serve food and refreshments to sick and wounded soldiers. They pitched in as assistants at dispensaries and helped in first aid stations. They were always ready for service.

As the war progressed, the Scouts were called on by the Government to perform numerous other services. They distributed thirty million pieces of literature. They sold close to half-a-billion-dollars worth of Liberty Loan Bonds and War Savings Stamps. They located twenty thousand board feet of black walnut for gun stocks and airplane propellers. They collected a hundred carloads of peach pits to be carbonized for use in gas masks. Wherever manpower could be replaced by boypower, the Scouts were prepared.

No wonder the Boy Scouts earned the respect of the country and were cited by the president for their work. No wonder thousands of boys wanted to become Scouts. And no wonder the Red Cross showed its appreciation of the Scouts by honoring them in its magazine. The organization went even further: it presented the original Rockwell paintings along with the engravers' plates from which they had been printed to the Boy Scouts of America.

The Boy Scouts made good use of these gifts. The paintings went on display in the national headquarters, where they were admired by all visitors. The plates were used for a series of *Boys' Life* covers and, soon after, for a set of prints sold through the National Supply Service, providing welcome revenue for the Boy Scout treasury.

The war ended with the armistice on the eleventh hour of the eleventh day of the eleventh month of 1918.

As soon as Norman was discharged, he got on the train for New Rochelle, walked straight home, slung his sea bag in the closet, and rushed out to look at his studio. There it was. "My studio. With my brushes upright in jars, my easel with '100%' in gold on its top, my comfortable old chair before it."

His first task was to get himself reestablished with the art directors of the major magazines. Did they want his work? They most certainly did. And so did the art directors for a number of major companies as well: Willys-Overland automobile company, Jell-O, Fisk bicycle tires, Orange Crush, Coca-Cola, Edison Mazda Lamp Works, and numerous others.

In the autumn of 1923 Norman took off for Europe. He haunted the streets and museums of Paris, then joined up with a newly married fellow artist and his wife for a swing around southern France and Italy: Marseilles, Monte Carlo, Florence, Venice, Milan. He sketched all the way and had a hilarious time.

Back in Paris, Norman enrolled in Colarossi's art school where Joseph Leyendecker had been a star student a number of years earlier. He felt completely at ease working at a realistic drawing of a model until another American student at the school stopped by. "You must have been born before 1860," he said, and walked off.

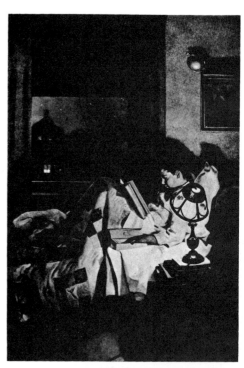

Norman's paintings for Edison Mazda were so well received that the company gave him a bonus of an all-expenses-paid "inspection tour" of its Caribbean agencies.

George Horace Lorimer, editor of the *Saturday Evening Post,* told Norman to charge twice as much for commercial art as he was being paid by the *Post.* Norman followed Lorimer's advice, and had as many advertising assignments as he could handle.

Some of Norman's friends back in New Rochelle had called his work "dated." He resolved to remedy the situation. He set out to learn about modern art and modern use of color. He attended lectures, visited art schools, tramped around from one avant-garde gallery to another, and decided upon his own kind of fling: he would paint two *Post* covers in the new style, each

Norman's dramatic new studio in New Rochelle, New York, had a large fireplace in one wall with a Windsor chair in front of it.

with some kind of symbolic figure—Winter as an old man in the cold colors of blues and icy gray, Spring as a young woman in the warm colors of yellow and apple green.

As soon as he got home, he went to work. When the Winter painting was finished, he took it down to the *Post*. Mr. Lorimer paced up and down before it for a long time, then stopped. "No!" he said. It was Norman's first rejection at the *Post*.

"This is not your kind of art," Lorimer said. "Your kind is what you have been doing all along. Stay with that." He added casually, "Now, what is your next cover for us going to be?"

Norman had eleven covers on the *Post* in 1924, nine the following year, and managed to do several pieces of advertising art besides.

His income kept growing. He bought himself a new house and built a spectacular and expensive studio behind it. The antique craze was on and the studio had to be Early American. He patterned it after the Wayside Inn in South Sudbury, Massachusetts. The outer walls were rough fieldstone; the inside walls were rough boards and beams. The floor boards were hand-hewn and wood-pegged. One wall had a brick fireplace with a fake balcony jutting out over it. The other walls were decorated with powder horns and bullet pouches, Revolutionary War muskets and steer horns.

If he had wanted to—and maybe he did—he could have hung on the wall the first of his fifty Boy Scout calendars, printed between 1925 and 1976. For now, at last, that very special project had come to fruition.

Fifty-Two Years of Boy Scout Calendars

For the first Norman Rockwell Boy Scout calendar, published in 1925, Brown & Bigelow used one of the pictures that Norman had painted for *The Red Cross Magazine* in 1918, with a different title from the original *A Red Cross Man in the Making*.

A GOOD SCOUT   1925

In 1923, some forgotten genius connected with the country's largest publisher of calendars, Brown & Bigelow of St. Paul, Minnesota, had a brainstorm.

The Boy Scouts of America had recently run a number of drives throughout the country for fund raising and recruiting Scout leaders and had succeeded in involving community leaders everywhere in their efforts. As part of their promotion, the Boy Scouts had made good use of their reproductions of the Rockwell Scout paintings commissioned by the Red Cross.

"Why not," reflected the Brown & Bigelow man, "tie the country's fastest growing youth movement to the production of a series of calendars that would appeal to every boy in the country, to fathers and mothers, to every past, present, and future Scout and Scout leader?"

At that time the calendar industry was not particularly noted for its contribution to aesthetic standards. Brown & Bigelow was something of an exception. The company had spared no expense to obtain the finest artists available for its calendars—artists such as Maxfield Parrish, Frank Hoffman, Andy Loomis, Dick Bishop, R. H. Palenske. Why not add Norman Rockwell to the list?

For the 1926 calendar, Norman submitted a number of ideas, sketched as usual on letterheads, pieces of drawing board, or tracing paper. He had just gone through a "circus period" during which he had painted a cover for *Life*, the old humor magazine, of a clown doing a good turn for a runaway boy *(left)*. Switching around the same idea, he depicted a Boy Scout doing a good turn for a circus acrobat, with a clown looking on.

A representative from Brown & Bigelow was sent to New York to meet with James E. West, the Chief Scout Executive, to present the company's proposal. The idea was to use one of the existing Rockwell paintings, the property of the Boy Scouts of America, for a calendar picture. There would be a great number of benefits to the Scouts in the project. The calendars would be sponsored by outstanding community firms and organizations that would give them a wide distribution. The image of Scouting would be on display before the public in stores and banks, in offices and work places, and in hundreds of thousands of homes. The advancement of Scouting would be greatly enhanced by such country-wide promotion. In addition, the Scouts would receive a royalty.

The Boy Scouts accepted the proposal.

Brown & Bigelow's art department got busy developing the 1925 calendar. They picked the Red Cross magazine illustra-

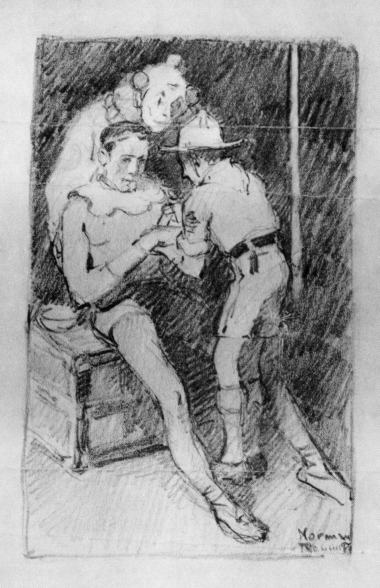

The Boy Scouts rejected Norman's circus picture in favor of the more conventional idea of a Scout reading to an old sailor.
A GOOD TURN   1926

tion showing a Scout bandaging the leg of a small dog. Their designers provided it with a frame made up of four pieces of rope, looped with overhand and figure-eight knots and tied together with square knots and sheetbends. They surrounded it with signal flags and merit badges, veterans' badges and medals. They changed the title from *A Red Cross Man in the Making* to *A Good Scout*. The company sent out promotional material to all prospective sponsors during the winter of 1923–24 and had its entire sales force on the road the following spring, covering the whole country.

Everyone at Brown & Bigelow foresaw a tremendous success that would call for an aggressive follow-up. Since the development of a calendar and its production spread over a two-year period, immediate planning for 1926 was imperative.

Brown & Bigelow came up with a double-feature plan: *Boys' Life* would arrange for a Norman Rockwell Scout painting well in advance, for its February 1926 cover. The same painting would then be used for the calendar of that year. This procedure would be followed in succeeding years.

Norman agreed to paint the cover for the February 1926 *Boys' Life* in the fall of 1924. He overwhelmed the Boy Scouts by telling them that he would do it without a fee, as "a labor of love." It would be an attempt to partially repay the Scouts for the start they had given him twelve years before. The following year he painted the February 1927 cover on the same basis. He missed the 1928 cover. He had too many other commitments in 1926 to make the deadline.

Norman's painting for 1929 was received with great enthusiasm. In addition to being used as the February *Boys' Life* cover and the Brown & Bigelow calendar picture, it served as the cover of the *Boy Scout Handbook* from 1927 to 1940, appearing on four million copies.

By this time, the Rockwell Boy Scout calendar had become an overwhelming success, and with it Brown & Bigelow led the calendar parade.

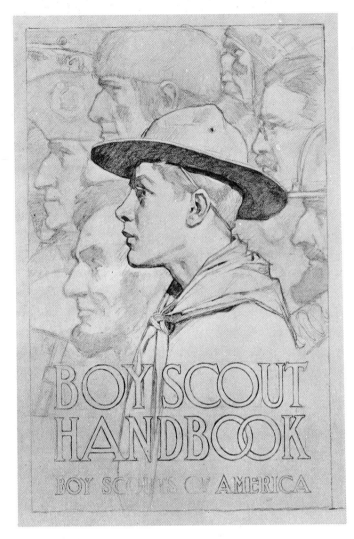

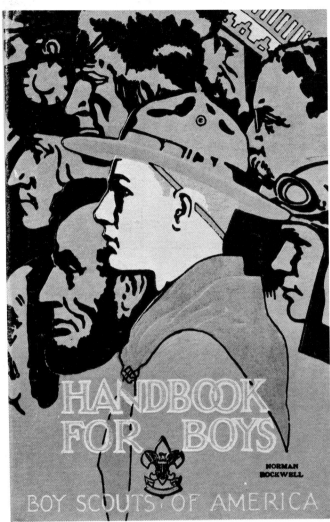

"Take the number ONE calendar of America, the number ONE artist, the number ONE boys' organization and the number ONE sales force and you have a combination that absolutely can't be beat," the company proclaimed.

The calendars were hanging on perhaps two million walls throughout the country. The sponsors who purchased them and sent them out to their customers and clients were many and varied: department stores, insurance agencies, oil companies, service stations, tire manufacturers, banks, savings and loan associations, pharmacies, drug stores, realtors, hardware stores, furniture stores, dairies, bowling lanes, funeral directors, soft drink manufacturers, ice cream companies, grocery stores.

The first four Boy Scout calendars had been produced in a rather casual way. Now, in 1928, Norman was not available to paint the picture for the 1930 calendar, which was supposed to

The painting for the 1929 calendar was also a *Boys' Life* cover and a cover for the new *Handbook for Boys*. Norman decided on a portrait of a Boy Scout against a background of characters from America's past: an Indian, a pioneer, a *conquistador*, Washington, Franklin, Lincoln, and Theodore Roosevelt. He had finished the charcoal sketch (*above, left*) when the country was stirred by the news of Charles Lindbergh's solo flight across the Atlantic. So, the *conquistador* went out and Lindbergh went in to represent, with the Scout, America's present and future. SPIRIT OF AMERICA 1929

A SCOUT IS LOYAL   1932

AN ARMY OF FRIENDSHIP   1933

CARRY ON   1934

A GOOD SCOUT   1935

The 1932 calendar painting paid tribute to George Washington on the two-hundredth anniversary of his birth.

1933 was the year of the Fourth Boy Scout World Jamboree, for which twenty-five thousand Scouts from all over the world were to gather in Hungary. In the foreground of the painting is a saluting American Scout. In the background are, clockwise, Scouts from Siam (now Thailand), Great Britain, Poland, Sudan, and Hungary, the latter with the traditional grass plume, the *Arvalanyhaj,* or "Orphan Maid's Hair," waving from his hat.

In the early thirties, the Boy Scouts of America were making an extra effort to hold the older Scouts in a special program. Hence the Senior Scout in the 1934 painting.

The always popular combination of "boy and dog" appears in 1935, with Senior Patrol Leader Robert West, son of the Chief Scout Executive, posing as the good Scout.

feature Dan Beard on his eightieth birthday. He was involved in too many other things. It became obvious that if the successful Scout calendars were to continue, more definite planning and a firm commitment would be necessary.

The procedure finally decided upon was quite simple:

James West, the Chief Scout Executive, would call in a couple of staff members with imagination and ask them to come up with a few ideas. He would present the ideas to Norman. Norman might have some counter-suggestions. Eventually, the two would agree on a theme. The Brown & Bigelow people would be informed and Norman would get on with the job.

While the work was in progress, West would send a knowledgeable staff member up to Norman's studio to check the painting. West expected absolute perfection. The Scout figure must represent American boyhood at its very best: he must be a clean-cut, wholesome youth—the pride and joy of every father and mother, a figure that every boy would want to emulate. His uniform must be immaculate no matter what tribulations he was

Norman (with sketches in his hands) discusses his calendar-picture ideas with members of the national staff of the Boy Scouts of America.

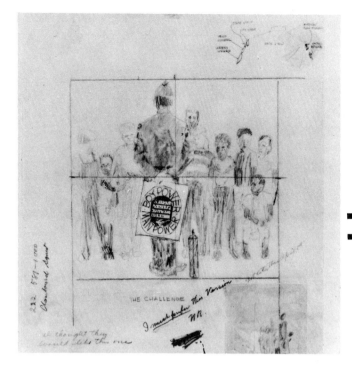

Norman made a special charcoal drawing for the promotion of the BOYPOWER-MANPOWER program in the 1970s. His early sketch *(top)* received the general approval of the national staff members involved in the program. His preliminary drawing *(center)* elicited a great number of suggestions by a large number of people. The final charcoal *(bottom)* was printed in an edition of three hundred copies, one hundred of which were selected and numbered. The rest, as well as the offset printing plate, were then destroyed.

The 1971 calendar painting is dedicated to the entire membership of the Boy Scouts of America. The nine-to-ten-year-old boys, with their blue and gold flag, represent the Cub Scouts. The khaki-clad boy holding a patrol flag stands for the Scouts, the green-clad young man for the Explorers. The den mother represents the female adult leaders. The men in back stand for adult, male leadership: national President, national Chief Scout Executive, local volunteer leader, local professional leader.
AMERICA'S MANPOWER BEGINS WITH BOYPOWER   1971

undergoing. The badges and insignia must be just right, the neckerchief tied correctly, the Scout hat slanted at the proper angle. The idealized figure might not be very true-to-life—but the viewer would love it.

By the time he brought in the finished picture, Norman's feelings about it would sometimes be approaching a slow boil.

West would put the painting on a chair in his office and call in a dozen staff members.

"What's wrong with it?" he would ask.

And, of course, they would find something wrong. "Shouldn't the father be a bit older?" "Isn't the boy to the left too pudgy?" "Wouldn't a red neckerchief be better?"

Fortunately, Norman was not a temperamental artist. If he had not been an understanding man, he might have been tempted to tell the staff members that the painting was the last he would do for the Scouts. Instead he let them talk. By the time these sessions ended, there had been so many contradictory suggestions that opinion had come full circle and the original picture was accepted with enthusiasm by everyone. Finally the painting was crated and shipped out to St. Paul.

In 1929 a new arrangement was made, reversing the previous one: the calendar firm would pay Norman for his paintings and would present them, after their reproduction, to the Boy Scouts of America. The Boy Scouts would then use the paintings for the February *Boys' Life* covers and in any other way they wished for other Scout publications and promotion pieces. Eventually, Norman's payment for a calendar painting was the equivalent of Gainsborough's fee for *The Blue Boy* and was more than forty times what Rembrandt received for the *Bathsheba* of 1654. The calendar fee surpassed even the very handsome renumeration that Norman was receiving for his *Post* covers.

In the mid-1930s a revolution was taking place in illustrating: It was caused by the introduction of the miniature 35-mm camera,

Posing a Norman Rockwell painting may involve more than a dozen people. Finding a suitable location, collecting the necessary paraphernalia, securing the Scout models and getting them correctly uniformed —all of this must be done before Norman arrives on the scene with his photographer and arranges the models.

To protect and improve the environment has been a Scouting objective from the beginning. But Scouting is also concerned with helping handicapped boys have a good boyhood—as Norman suggests by including a crutch in his calendar painting *(right)*.
SO MUCH CONCERN   1975

which took so-called candid photographs. Up to that time, the use of photography had been frowned upon among artists. Now that very natural poses were possible, it became an accepted procedure to paint from photographs of models instead of painting from them directly.

Norman resisted the use of the camera longer than many artists. It was a struggle. It took him three or four days, with his models posing five or six hours a day, to paint a figure. Only professional models were able to work that many hours, and the right types were difficult to find. The same model could not be used again and again. Many stopped modeling for artists and took more lucrative jobs. The younger ones could earn more posing for a photographer.

Having the models hold their poses was another major difficulty. Norman would be ready to drop after sitting for five hours or more, yelling at a model to "Raise the arm an inch!" or

right: Norman sometimes had trouble getting his models to understand what poses he wanted them to take. So, rather than trying to describe the poses and expressions he desired, he acted them out. This often involved him in acrobatic contortions, but the models then knew exactly what Norman had in mind and could imitate his actions.

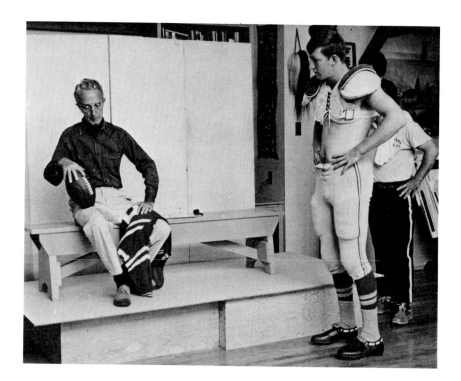

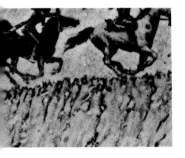

left: Posing a model sitting on a bench was not hard. Here the main point would be to show just how the athlete should sit and how he should handle the props included in the picture.

"Lift the eyebrows!" or "Smile a little wider!" The models themselves were often ready to give up.

Henry Quinan, who served in the course of his career as the art director of *American* magazine, *Collier's*, and *Woman's Home Companion,* set Norman off on the trail of using photographs about 1937. It didn't take him long to develop his own technique.

After deciding on his story idea, he made his usual small preliminary sketch of the action he planned to show, the composition he had in mind, the poses of the characters. He then collected the props needed to set the stage: costumes and accessories, equipment and furniture. When all was ready he brought in the models and his photographer. In posing the models, Norman demonstrated the positions he wanted them to take and the gestures and expressions he wanted them to hold. When he was satisfied that he had all the photos he needed, he dismissed his models.

The following day he spread out on the floor 8-by-10-inch prints of the shots the photographer had taken. From these he selected what he wanted: a particularly well-held pose, the position of an arm in another shot, the slant of a head in a third, a broad smile in a fourth. With his preliminary sketch in front of him to guide him and the selected photographs to help him, he now made one or more small pencil sketches. When one of them

finally satisfied him, he put it into his Balopticon—a mechanical device for projecting opaque, flat subjects such as photographs and drawings. He projected it onto a sheet of architect's paper, blowing it up to the size he intended for the final painting, and then traced the picture in great detail in charcoal.

The next step was to settle on the colors. Norman had his photographer copy his charcoal layout and prepare a couple of matte prints, 8-by-10-inches or slightly larger in size. On these he worked out his color scheme in oil.

For the actual painting, he started by placing a sheet of semitransparent architect's tracing paper over the charcoal drawing and tracing the whole picture on it in pencil. He then placed a sheet of transfer paper on the canvas, put the tracing on top of it, and transferred the drawing to the canvas. Finally, the brushwork: a monochromatic underpainting, then a rapid "laying-in" of colors followed by painting, in oil, the figures of

Sometimes Norman might paint one or more color sketches of a background scene, then paint a foreground figure on an acetate overlay (above). Notice, in two sketches below, that the standing figure under the tent flap became a seated figure and that the cross-bar pot hanger over the campfire disappeared.

his composition with all the details that would make the result a true "Norman Rockwell."

By 1938 twenty-five years had passed since Norman Rockwell had joined the national staff of the Boy Scouts of America as the sole artist for *Boys' Life*. Throughout these years, he had been a true friend of Scouting and had done much to popularize the Scout movement, its activities, and its ideals.

That winter, at the meeting of the Court of Honor Committee of the Boy Scouts' executive board, a unanimous decision was reached. Norman Rockwell was to be awarded the highest award of the Boy Scouts of America: the Silver Buffalo presented to men who had rendered distinguished service to the nation's boys—the same award that had earlier been given to Baden-Powell, Ernest Thompson Seton, Dan Beard, and other outstanding leaders in the work for boys.

The presentation took place the following spring at the Boy Scouts' twenty-ninth annual meeting in New York City.

Norman improved the composition of the patrol at its camp meal by making the patrol leader in the foreground larger and changing his position so that he did not obscure any of the seated Scouts.
WE THANK THEE, O' LORD 1974

 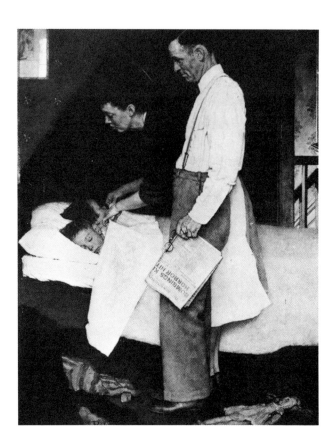

The lights had been dimmed in the main ballroom of the Waldorf-Astoria when Norman, with five other prominent American citizens, was called up on the stage to receive the award before an audience of nearly three thousand people. The chairman of the National Court of Honor read the citation:

Norman Rockwell, artist, distinguished delineator of Boy Scouts and of boyhood.

To the people of America he has brought a deepened understanding of the psychology of boys of Scout age.

At the very outset of his career he became an illustrator for *Boys' Life* in the first year of its publication by the Boy Scouts of America. He gave the joy and inspiration of Scouting ideals to hundreds of thousands of youthful citizens of the nation.

He has assisted the Boy Scout movement through his interpretive paintings of flesh-and-blood boys and has helped to win the American people to an appreciation of the fundamentals of Scouting.

A smartly-uniformed Scout carried in the Silver Buffalo award on a velvet cushion. The chairman of the Court of Honor hung the award, by its red-and-white ribbon, around Norman's neck. The audience rose in a standing ovation.

The Four Freedoms, illustrating President Franklin D. Roosevelt's four essentials for human happiness, are among Rockwell's most famous paintings. *Freedom of Speech, Freedom from Fear, Freedom of Worship,* and *Freedom from Want* were used during World War II to sell war bonds—over $130 million worth.

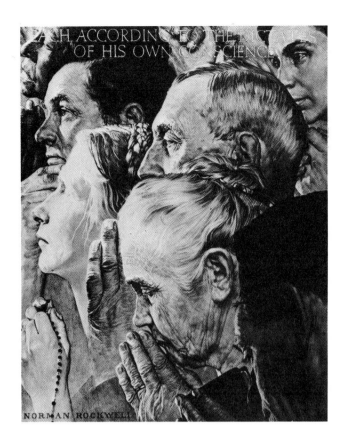

These typical Americans, to whom their countrymen responded with such warmth, were Norman's Vermont neighbors, pressed into service as artists' models for this most ambitious and inspired undertaking. The paintings hang today in the Corner House at Stockbridge, Massachusetts, a museum of Rockwell memorabilia.

The Norman Rockwell family—which now included three sons—Jerry, Tommy, and Peter—moved to Arlington, Vermont in 1939. The decision was right. Vermont promised a different kind of life. Norman would get new inspiration. The boys would have a wonderful childhood roaming the country.

The first year, to the Vermonters around them, the Rockwells were summer people, transients. The next year they were accepted members of the community. Norman met a hundred or more people he wanted to paint. Everyone seemed willing and eager to pose. His imagination took on new life: "Ideas were jumping in my brain like trout on the Batten Kill at sunset. I'd found what I wanted—new people, new surroundings."

On September 1, 1939, Hitler's armies invaded Poland—the start of World War II.

On January 6, 1941, President Franklin D. Roosevelt appeared before Congress and enunciated the Four Freedoms which he deemed essential for human happiness: Freedom of Speech and Expression, Freedom of Worship, Freedom from Want, and Freedom from Fear. Norman kept turning over the thought of these freedoms in his mind. They gave him no peace until he had caught their spirit in four magnificent paintings. These were done over a period of six months using his Vermont neighbors for his models. The *Post* published the pictures on its

inside pages, each accompanied by an essay by a well-known American writer.

The four paintings appeared at a time when the war that the United States had joined after Pearl Harbor was going against America on all battlefronts, when the American people needed the inspiration they provided.

The paintings quickly became the best known and most highly appreciated pictures of the war years. They were reprinted on millions of posters and distributed throughout America and the world. The originals were sent on a country-wide tour and were instrumental in selling millions of dollars worth of war bonds.

Norman was still trying to recover from the intense creative effort of painting the Four Freedoms when he completed the long overdue Boy Scout calendar picture for 1944. This, too, had an inspirational appeal. It showed a strong American boy saluting and declaring, "We, too, have a job to do." Norman wrapped up the finished painting and sent it off to Brown & Bigelow one afternoon.

That night his studio burned to the ground.

He lost an irreplaceable collection of costumes, reference materials, sketches, paintings, antiques. He took the incident in his stride, turning it into a double-page spread for the July 17, 1943, issue of the *Post:* "My Studio Burns Down." He fitted out his next studio with fire extinguishers and other fire-fighting equipment.

Coming up with ideas for the yearly Scout calendar was getting more and more complicated. It was turning into a time-consuming, hurdle-filled process.

In the early years it had not been too hard to picture a Boy Scout in action representing the Scouting program. But in the thirties and forties the Boy Scouts of America had come up with two other programs: Cub Scouting for younger boys, Senior Scouting—Sea Scouting, Air Scouting, and eventually

With a much larger membership than during World War I, the Boy Scouts of America were able to do an even greater job in World War II. Many American men who fought in the war in the field often survived because of their early Scout training. Meanwhile, young Scouts at home served by collecting aluminum and rubber, acting as dispatch bearers and fire watchers for Civil Defense, distributing air-raid and war-bond posters and pamphlets, and raising food in victory gardens. The figure of a First Class Scout, posed before the American flag with his hand raised in the three-finger Scout salute that stands for the three parts of the Scout Oath, expressed the dedication of the Boy Scouts to the American cause.

WE, TOO, HAVE A JOB TO DO 1944

Exploring—for older boys. The staff members promoting each of these programs felt that their branch should be represented on the calendar picture.

But how to show Cub Scouts, Boy Scouts, and Explorers in action together—that was the rub. They could be sitting together in a pew. They could be walking together. They could be participating in some family activity. Too often, however, the result was the safe picture of everybody standing around like statues, doing nothing.

Another problem was that having to paint several figures instead of just one invariably upset Norman's always optimistic schedule.

Norman had suffered from the tyranny of deadlines throughout his career. "A deadline is like a mean-tempered terrier," he said once, "It won't leave you alone for a minute. You run and hide behind a tree and after a while, thinking you've escaped him, you step out and . . . *rowf!* he's got you by the heel." As time went by Norman became "pretty casual" about deadlines.

But this would not do for Claire Frye, the art director of Brown & Bigelow, who worked with Norman for thirty-three years getting his annual calendar art to "bed." The trouble with Claire was that he knew when a deadline died.

"It wasn't Norman's fault that it was hard for him to deliver on time," Claire explained later. "It was due to the tremendous pressure of his work. He just couldn't say 'No' to anyone, so he promised more than he could possibly deliver. But at Brown & Bigelow the production schedule was almost a religion—it had to be when press time was worked out on an almost split-second plan to handle all the different sizes of calendars of each of our fifty accounts. So I was in hot water every year when the Scout painting was due."

Norman and Claire went out west together in 1953 when the Boy Scouts were holding their third national jamboree at the Irvine Ranch in southern California. The event was attended by

With the Boy Scouts of America branched out into three separate programs, it became hard for Norman to come up with ideas that included all three. One solution consisted of putting representatives of the three branches into a group picture such as this, showing a Boy Scout senior patrol leader with his hand on the shoulder of a Cub Scout, and with three other figures representing the three phases of the senior program: Exploring, Air Scouting, and Sea Scouting.
FORWARD AMERICA 1951

45,000 Scouts from all parts of the United States and from twenty-one countries around the world. Norman wanted to see the Scouts in action at a jamboree, and also planned to get photos for his next calendar painting. He had a special idea in mind: he was going to dedicate the picture to the American Scoutmaster. "Those Scoutmasters truly have something," he said. "I have admired their skill as I have watched them work with boys. Talk about good Americans doing things for their community—they're doing it."

Norman reaped several extra dividends from his western trip. On the way back from California he and Claire stopped in New Mexico for a jaunt to the Philmont Scout Ranch where Norman did research for his 1957 calendar.

A quick trip into the nearby village of Cimarron gave Norman the idea for a *Post* cover. It was a combination of an old pick-up truck, an old rancher, and his son that clicked in his mind. The picture he painted, *Breaking Home Ties,* was one of his most thought-provoking: two figures sitting on the running

In 1953 Norman went to the Third National Jamboree of the Boy Scouts of America, at Irvine Ranch in California, to paint a calendar picture of the most important adult leader in Scouting, the Scoutmaster. He arranged for a troop to put up a suitable camp, then hunted around for a model. He found him at jamboree headquarters: Marshall Ammerman, a jamboree coordinator and former Scoutmaster. It was only after the painting was finished that the Boy Scout camping experts discovered the tents were the frowned-upon war surplus "pups." The problem was taken care of by painting a low sidewall and guy ropes on one of the offending tents. This is one of the most popular and inspiring of all the Rockwell Scout paintings.

THE SCOUTMASTER 1956

above: One of Norman's finest *Saturday Evening Post* covers, *Breaking Home Ties*, 1954

After the jamboree Norman stopped at the Philmont Scout Ranch, the high-adventure national Scout reservation of close to 140,000 Rocky Mountain acres in New Mexico. As many as 15,000 campers a year travel into the mountain fastnesses of Philmont for one of the most thrilling adventures of their Scouting lives. Norman's painting shows Explorers hiking and climbing, toting packs and leading burros, with the "Tooth of Time," a granite cliff that towers over the plain below, looming in the background.
HIGH ADVENTURE 1957

board of a beat-up truck, waiting for the train that would carry the boy off to college—a father thinking of the past and of his son growing up, a boy dreaming of the future.

By the time the picture appeared on the cover of the *Post* (September 25, 1954), the Rockwells had pulled up stakes and had moved to Stockbridge, Massachusetts.

The early fifties had been hectic years for Norman. The late fifties were even more so. In addition to covers for the *Post* and Boy Scout and Four Seasons calendars for Brown & Bigelow, he was painting cards for Hallmark and doing advertising art for half a dozen companies. The year 1959 broke all records for the number of deadlines Norman had to meet.

The fiftieth birthday of the Boy Scouts of America was fast approaching. It would be celebrated with great fanfare in 1960.

In preparation for the Golden Jubilee, a brand-new, spectacular *Boy Scout Handbook* was planned. It would have a first printing of a million copies, an all-time high, and would need a very special cover. Norman's famous cover for the 1927 edition and his subsequent Scout paintings left no doubt that he was the artist who could best express the spirit of Scouting.

Norman agreed to make the suggested cover painting of an entire Scout patrol in camp. Other commitments were clamoring for execution. His health wasn't too good. He was on the verge of giving up on the *Handbook* cover, but changed his mind. He could not undertake the elaborate scene that had been proposed, but he would do a single outline figure of a hiking Scout. Some other artist would have to provide the background. The painting arrived just in time to be rushed to the engraver. The Rockwell cover appeared on three-and-a-half-million copies of the new *Boy Scout Handbook*.

When a new *Handbook for Boys* was being prepared for the Golden Anniversary of Scouting in 1960, the book's art director, Don Ross, and its author, William Hillcourt, agreed that Norman was the logical artist to do the cover. The awkward pose in the first painting *(below)* was later corrected for the handbook cover.

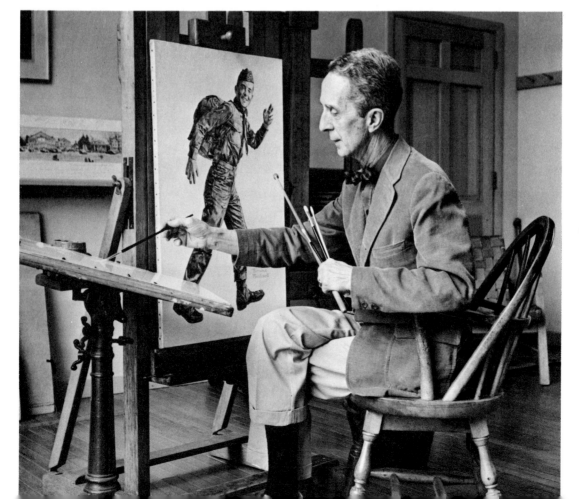

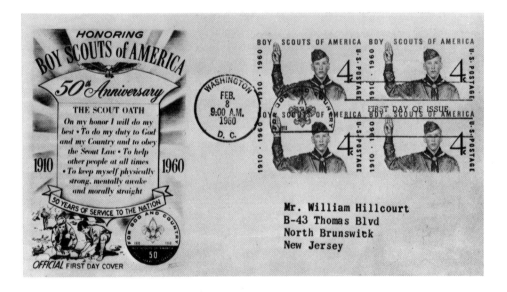

Mr. William Hillcourt
B-43 Thomas Blvd
North Brunswick
New Jersey

There was another Scout-related job that Norman had agreed to do—this one at Government request. The Boy Scouts of America had persuaded the Post Office to bring out a commemorative stamp in celebration of its jubilee. And who should do the art work? Norman Rockwell, of course. He managed to submit the design in the nick of time.

In the 1960s the world was changing rapidly and the magazine world was changing along with it. The *Saturday Evening Post* suspended publication with its issue of February 8, 1969. *Look* folded on October 16, 1971. Of the many magazines for which Norman had worked during his long career only one remained: *Boys' Life,* the publication in which he had started his career,

Norman's color sketches for a calendar picture to show the world brotherhood of Scouting and to promote the 1967 World Jamboree did not quite come off. A color photograph from the 1963 World Jamboree in Greece saved the day. In painting the picture Norman changed the uniforms to represent all parts of the world.
BREAKTHROUGH FOR
FREEDOM 1967

was still going strong, with more than two million subscribers— the figure that had so impressed Norman in 1916 when that many copies of his first *Post* cover were printed.

Norman's Scout calendar paintings of the late sixties and early seventies reflect some of the same preoccupations as the illustrations he did for *Look* magazine in those years: friendship among the youth of the world, Scouts of all races having fun together in their patrols and troops, conserving the nation's resources, keeping the faith in America.

During this period, the procedure of having the Boy Scouts, Brown & Bigelow, and Norman jointly decide on the theme for the yearly calendar was broken once. The subject of the 1969 calendar was *dictated* to Norman. He had no choice in the matter. He had to accept the idea and perform.

For over forty years, Norman had honored the Boy Scouts

For the 1969 calendar, the national staff of the Boy Scouts of America and the Brown & Bigelow representatives plotted together to celebrate Norman's seventy-fifth birthday. They insisted on a painting of Norman himself surrounded by a group of Scouts like those he had been painting for so many years *(left)*.
BEYOND THE EASEL   1969

Norman took the inspiration for his last calendar picture, intended to celebrate the two-hundredth anniversary of the Declaration of Independence, from the famous painting *Spirit of '76* by Archibald M. Willard. Norman revised his preliminary sketch *(left)* to add an extra Explorer carrying the American flag of 1976, with its fifty stars, and an adult leader beckoning other boys to join in Scouting's onward march.
THE SPIRIT OF 1976   1976

with a painting for use as the February birthday cover of *Boys' Life*. Now it was Norman's turn to be honored, with a Scout calendar to celebrate his seventy-fifth birthday.

Although he had previously included himself in many of his pictures, this was the first time he was required to make himself the focal character of one of his paintings.

In 1974, when he was eighty, Norman announced that his 1976 Scout calendar painting would be his last.

He picked for his theme "The Spirit of '76" and for his composition the famous painting by Archibald M. Willard. But he changed the original revolutionary figures into a Cub Scout, a Scout, and an Explorer. The painting was Norman's final salute to the Boy Scouts of America and his contribution to the celebration of the Bicentennial of the Declaration of Independence of the United States of America.

Norman Rockwell's Scout work is finished but his fame endures.

Norman Rockwell and the Ideals of Scouting

The fifty calendar pictures and other Scout pictures that Norman painted over a period of almost sixty years were aimed at catching the attention of Scouts and of boys not yet Scouts, of their parents, and of the public at large. Their purpose was to excite everyone about Scouting and its potential. In each picture, he incorporated some aspect of the fundamentals of the Scout movement.

What are those fundamentals? The founder of Scouting expressed them quite simply and reiterated them again and again in his writings. His thoughts became the basis for Scouting around the world.

"Scouting," Baden-Powell said, "is a game for boys, under the leadership of boys, in which elder brothers can give their younger brothers a healthy environment and encourage them to healthy activities such as will help them develop CITIZENSHIP."

A game, then, but what kind of game? Baden-Powell gave the explanation: "By the term 'Scouting' is meant the work and attributes of backwoodsmen, explorers, hunters, seamen, airmen, pioneers, and frontiersmen. To give the elements of these to boys, Scouting supplies a system of games and practices

Even the indoor activities of the troop meeting room or the patrol den are "outdoorsy"—aimed at preparing each Scout for his hiking and camping adventures. In this painting, Norman shows a troop taking off for a camping expedition. But he also tells another story. Look closer. Follow the hand-wave of the Scout under the sign. To whom is he waving? To a kid in the window above, dreaming of the day when he will be old enough to join the Scouts.
SCOUTING IS OUTING   1968

which meet their desires and instincts, and appeal to their imagination and romance." Scouting provides the boys with an active outdoor life. It gives them a chance to wear an attractive uniform and grants them recognition for mastering various skills. It holds before them the ideals of a true Scout and encourages them to "help other people at all times."

"Scouting is a brotherhood." Baden-Powell emphasized this point. "It is a scheme which, in practice, disregards differences of class, creed, country, and color."

A big order—but not too big if Scouting is to accomplish its aims of "building desirable qualities of character, of training boys in the responsibilities of participating citizenship, of developing their physical fitness."

"Scouting is a game for boys under the leadership of boys." In Scouting, the boys are formed into small groups—patrols. They elect a member of their group to be their leader under whom they pursue their Scouting activities in their own special way.

Baden-Powell stressed the importance of the patrol in Scouting. "The patrol is the unit of Scouting always, whether for work or play, for discipline or duty. The patrol method . . . is the

MEN OF TOMORROW   1948

GROWTH OF A LEADER   1966

one essential feature in which Scout training differs from that of all other organizations. Where the method is properly applied, it is absolutely bound to bring success. It cannot help itself!"

Norman idealized the American patrol leader in his painting *Tomorrow's Leader* (1959).* The Scout portrayed is a strong character, physically fit, a leader of vision and determination. Norman shows him prepared and ready to guide his patrol with the aid of the handbook and compass he holds. He suggests the patrol leader's skills by the First Class badge and the merit badges behind him.

He shows the patrol leader in action in other paintings: moving the patrol out of the troop meeting room for a camping trip (1968), getting ready for a meal in camp (1974), leading his patrol in a portage on a waterways expedition (1948). And he shows the development of a boy as a leader from his earliest days in Scouting until he reaches manhood (1966).

But Norman knew that the patrol leaders succeed mainly through the training given them by their Scoutmaster (1962). It

*With the exception of 1918, the dates refer to the year when the Rockwell painting appeared on the Scout calendar. With the exception of the 1925 calendar, Norman painted the Scout pictures two years before.

left: The dedicated Scoutmaster, thoroughly trained for his task, sets the tone of the troop. He points the way and guides his boys toward citizenship by inspiring them to master the skills of Scouting and challenging them to live up to the Scout Oath and Law to which they have pledged themselves.
POINTING THE WAY   1962

right: The campfire is the heart of the Scout camp. The memories of campfire flames, songs, and laughter, and silent gazing into dying embers will stay with the boys for many years to come. To the leader the campfire offers a golden opportunity to instill in his boys the ideals of Scouting.
THE CAMPFIRE STORY   1936

is the devotion of the Scoutmaster and his planning for the future, even after his charges have turned in for the night (1956), that makes Scouting successful.

Adventure in the outdoors—that's why boys become Scouts. There's excitement to Scouting—hiking and camping. There's joy to it. The very word *camp* stands for freedom, fun, and adventure: it suggests tents under the open sky, bacon sizzling in the pan, days full of thrilling action, sitting with your best friends at night around a blazing campfire.

    In one of his earliest Scout pictures, Norman painted that last scene: a troop of Scouts sitting around a campfire listening to

Cooking was proposed as the theme for the 1970 calendar painting. Norman made several suggestions, one of them with a humorous slant: "Grandmother's Recipe" *(above)*. It was finally decided to make cooking incidental to a troop camp picture, with a Scoutmaster awaiting the arrival of the patrols. The setting is a small island in Lake Therese at the Schiff Scout Reservation, the national training center of the Boy Scouts of America near Mendham, New Jersey.

COME AND GET IT! 1970

a yarn their Scoutmaster is spinning (1918). Norman repeated the same idea many years later, but gave the Scoutmaster a smaller audience. He focused attention on the adult leader, without whose determination and support a Scout might never have his camping experience (1936).

There are many forms of camping, as Norman shows in his paintings.

Camping can be the simple action of a single patrol (1974) or a larger encampment of the whole troop (1970). It can be a traveling camp, using canoes for transportation (1948) or even a trek over the mountains of the Philmont Scout Ranch with packs and burros, with the goal the distinctive peak called The Tooth of Time (1957).

In his paintings, Norman managed to cover a great number of other special activities of Scouting. Orienting oneself by compass, for instance (1959, '62), map reading (1943), cooking (1970, '74), knot-tying (1946), pioneering and signaling (1918), first aid—specifically to animals (1925, '49), canoeing (1948), rock-climbing (1947), Indian lore (1936, '52), handicraft (1938, '55). The depiction of these Scoutcraft skills demonstrates yet another of Scouting's fundamentals: learning by doing.

SCOUTS OF MANY TRAILS 1937

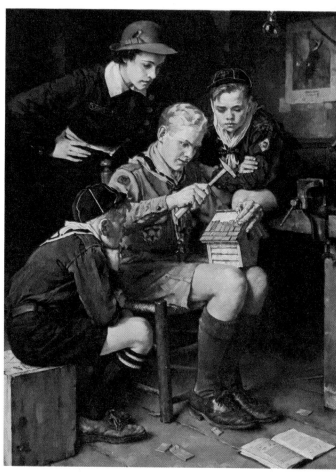

AMERICA BUILDS FOR TOMORROW 1938

A SCOUT IS FRIENDLY 1943

A GUIDING HAND 1946

FRIEND IN NEED   1949

THE ADVENTURE TRAIL   1952

Norman depicted a great number of Scoutcraft skills in his many paintings. It is easy enough to identify the skills suggested in these seven pictures—but go beyond the obvious and use the pictures for a game of observation, to find some of the scarcely noticeable details that Norman always includes: the sextant in the sea chest in the 1937 picture, the ship model on the wall, the map of St. John, Virgin Islands, on the table. Notice in the 1938 picture that the Scout's badges indicate that he is a member of the Fox patrol and was a participant in the First National Jamboree. In the 1943 picture, the leader of the Eagle patrol is well prepared, with a knife at his belt and a whistle in his pocket, as indicated by the lanyard around his neck. In the 1946 picture, what knot is the First Class Scout teaching the Cub Scout of Den 6? And in the 1949 picture, to what patrol does the Scout belong and how many years has the younger boy been a Cub Scout? Do you realize that the First Class Scout, a six-year veteran, in the 1952 picture, is not only a senior patrol leader in his Scout troop but also a den chief in a Cub Scout pack? And after you looked at the action in the 1955 picture, did you notice the knot board behind the Star Scout?

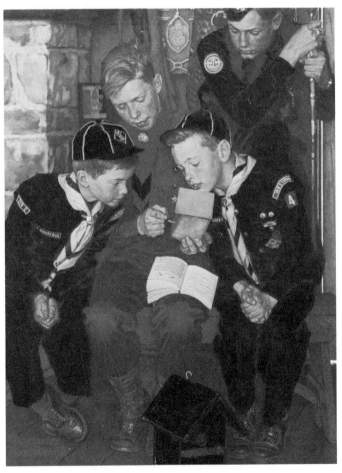

THE RIGHT WAY   1955

The Scout uniform and the Scout badges belong together. The uniform shows that a boy is a member of the world brotherhood of Scouting. The badges he adds to the uniform are in recognition of the leadership he is giving, the service he has rendered, the skills he has mastered.

Norman, from time to time, might have had problems depicting the multitude of activities that Scouting has to offer. He never had any problems in regard to illustrating uniforms and badges. The specifications are spelled out precisely in the Scout literature, and his early training under Chief West, a near-fanatic on the subject of correct uniform, stood him in good stead for all the pictures he painted later.

By grouping together a number of Norman's paintings depicting Scouts in their uniforms, it is possible to follow the various stages of Scouting, as symbolized by the changing uniform.

The Cub Scout who just "Can't Wait!" (1972) has shed his blue Cub Scout uniform and has donned his older brother's oversize khaki Boy Scout outfit. He looks at himself in the mirror and imagines all the fun he is going to have as a full-fledged Boy Scout.

Before long, the youngster reaches the required age for becoming a Boy Scout. With the help of his brother, an

In his hopeful smile and eager bearing, the Cub Scout looking in the mirror expresses the longings and expectations of the ten-year-old as he dreams of becoming a Scout. The preliminary sketches (above) show the steps that Norman took in developing his painting. In the final version, notice particularly the picture on the wall and the relocation of the dog, who calls attention to the mirror.
CAN'T WAIT   1972

"Can't Wait!"

Norman materially changed the composition and the details of his 1961 calendar painting between the original sketch and the final version.

Explorer, and with an assist from his mother he gets into his own uniform, while his father approves and his younger brother looks on enviously (1958). Soon after, the badges of leadership, service, and achievement begin to sprout on the boy's uniform.

Some of Norman's Scouts demonstrate by their badges that they have become patrol leaders (1943, '48, '49). Others have reached the office of senior patrol leader (1935, '51, '60); still others have helped in Cub Scouting as den chiefs (1947, '50, '60). Some show by their service stars that they have been Scouts for two years (1933, '42), for three years (1944), even for six years and more (1954, '66). Some have reached the rank of First Class Scout (1942, '45, '54, '55, '61), one the rank of Star Scout (1955).

The ultimate goal in Scouting is to become an Eagle Scout. In addition to showing an Eagle Scout in a couple of his paintings (1936, '60), Norman painted the ceremony in which a boy is awarded this coveted badge (1965). Arriving at Eagle rank is

"He went to camp a boy, he came home a man." That has often been the experience of a Scout who has lived the kind of life in the open that a well-run summer camp provides. In such a camp the Scout builds up his health and strength. He learns to be resourceful, self-reliant. His love for his land and its nature deepens. He learns to get along with others, to do his share in the patrol for the common good. He picks up the skills of outdoor cooking and pioneering, hiking and orienteering, swimming and lifesaving, boating and canoeing.
HOMECOMING 1961

not a lonely pursuit. It is hard work for the Scout himself. But he is helped by the inspiration and expectations of a dedicated Scoutmaster and, often, by the pushing of a father and the prodding of a mother. The mother's expression of obvious pride and relief as she finally pins the badge on her son's uniform reflects Norman's appreciation of her contribution to the Scout's achievement.

MIGHTY PROUD   1958

A GREAT MOMENT   1965

There is a dream in the heart of every new Scout, as he dons his uniform for the first time, that, one of these days, he will reach the peak in Scouting and become an Eagle Scout. Those who make it to Eagle have an experience and training that will benefit them for the rest of their lives.

The ideals of Scouting are expressed in the Scout Oath to which a boy pledges himself on becoming a Scout, when he raises his right hand in the Scout sign, the middle fingers upward, the thumb touching the little finger—the universal symbol of Scouting throughout the world.
I WILL DO MY BEST   1945

ON MY HONOR   1953

Of all the phases of Scouting, Norman paid the greatest attention to the spirit of the movement as expressed in its ideals—the Scout Oath and the Scout Law.

On becoming a Scout, a boy pledges to fulfill the SCOUT OATH:

> On my honor, I will do my best
> To do my duty to God and my country and to obey
>   the Scout Law;
> To help other people at all times,
> To keep myself physically strong, mentally awake, and
>   morally straight.

In two of his paintings (1945, '53) Norman shows a Scout making his solemn pledge, with the Oath emblazoned on the wall behind him.

He covered the details of the Scout Oath in several paintings: duty to God in pictures of boys involved in their religious observances (1940, '54); duty to country in seven patriotic tableaux (1929, '32, '42, '44, '50, '73, '76), and living the Scout Law in a whole series of paintings.

"Helping other people at all times" through the performance of the "daily good turn" is the theme of several of Norman's pictures. One of his earliest paintings shows a Boy Scout helping an elderly man across a crowded city street (1918). Other paintings depict the Scout assisting an elderly couple in finding their way in a strange town (1943), helping a Cub Scout learn to tie the Tenderfoot knots that will open the door of Scouting to him (1946), and helping Cub Scouts with their handicraft projects (1938, '55).

In some of his paintings, Norman indicated a Scout doing his "duty to God" by showing him taking part in religious services.
A SCOUT IS REVERENT   1954

In his 1950 calendar painting (*right*), Norman combined "duty to God" and "duty to country" in a single picture. There was an extra significance to this painting: that year more than fifty thousand Scouts took part in the Second National Boy Scout Jamboree at Valley Forge, Pennsylvania, where Washington had prayed during the dark days of the winter of 1777–78.
OUR HERITAGE   1950

Physical fitness has been one of the aims of the Scout movement from its inception. By participating regularly and enthusiastically in all the vigorous activities that Scouting has to offer, a Scout can't help but add to his strength and general health.
ALL TOGETHER   1947

A more humorous approach to physical fitness is seen in the picture of an earnest body-builder *(right)* whose younger brother is helping to measure his expanded chest.
TO KEEP MYSELF PHYSICALLY
STRONG   1964

The Scout's adherence to the third part of the Scout Oath is implied in a number of Norman's paintings.

Certainly, his depiction of rugged activities suggests the benefits derived from them that keep the Scout "physically strong." The same subject is covered in one of the few Scout paintings to which Norman gave a humorous slant (1964). In this picture a Cub Scout is seen measuring his older Scout brother's still scrawny chest. The "mentally awake" aspect of the Scout Oath is suggested in paintings showing Scouts mastering their Scoutcraft skills, the "morally straight" pledge in pictures illustrating the points of the Scout Law.

The SCOUT LAW that a Scout tries to follow consists of twelve points:

A Scout is Trustworthy, Loyal, Helpful, Friendly, Courteous, Kind, Obedient, Cheerful, Thrifty, Brave, Clean, Reverent.

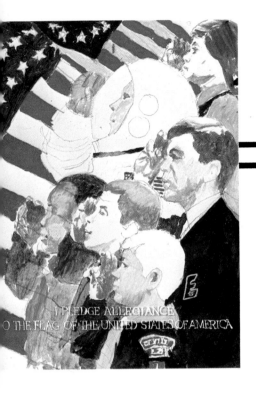

Norman managed to depict most of these qualities directly, by title, in his paintings.

To express "Trustworthy," "Loyal," and "Obedient," Norman generally placed the Scout in a patriotic setting, with the flag of his country (1944, '73, '76) or the symbolic figures of his country's leaders (1932, '42, '50) behind him.

"Helpful" and "Courteous" are treated in his many illustrations of a Scout performing his "daily good turn."

Every painting that shows a happy Scout in company with

Norman's inspiring painting *(left)* appeared at a time when the loyalty of all Americans was put to the test by the entry of the United States into World War II.
A SCOUT IS LOYAL   1942

The rather obscure and poetic title of the 1973 calendar *(right)* refers to locations where two revolutions began: the American revolution at Concord, Massachusetts, and the space-age "revolution" at the landing site on the moon: the "Sea of Tranquility." Nine of the ten Americans who walked on the moon were Scouts as boys; the first, Neil A. Armstrong, was an Eagle Scout.
FROM CONCORD TO TRANQUILITY   1973

his brother Scouts of his own country or other countries (1933,
'63, '67) expresses the "Friendly" and "Cheerful" points of the
Scout Law.

"A Scout is Kind" was one of Norman's favorites, and a
number of his pictures dealt with kindness to animals in particular. He knew that the combination of a dog and a boy would
have great general appeal. His very first Scout calendar painting shows a Scout bandaging the leg of a small puppy (1925). He
used the same idea in a picture executed many years later
(1949). Another picture shows a Scout demonstrating his kindness by giving water to a thirsty dog in its crate in a freight
station (1935), and there is one of a Scout feeding a whole litter
(1927).

"A Scout is Brave" is implied in several of Norman's paintings showing the daring activities in which Scouts participate. A
specific example is the picture of a Scout rescuing a small girl
caught in a flood (1941).

"Clean" and "Reverent"—cleanliness of thought, rever-
ence for his Maker. Norman combined these points of the Scout

Law in two paintings: one of a single Scout (1940), the other of a grouping of a Cub Scout, a Boy Scout, and an Explorer (1954) at religious services.

Finally, in three of the most colorful Scout pictures he ever painted, Norman expressed the real spirit of the Scout movement by vividly depicting the concept of World Brotherhood that is the basis of Scouting (1933, '63, '67).

Truly, Norman Rockwell was the delineator of the best that Scouting has to offer. He proved himself a good Scout and a true friend of Scouting—not just to the boys of his own country but to boyhood around the globe.

To suggest the twelfth point of the Scout Law, "A Scout is Reverent," Norman painted a First Class Scout kneeling in a church pew next to an elderly parishioner (left).
A SCOUT IS REVERENT   1940

In Norman's 1963 painting, dedicated to the world brotherhood of Scouting, a Scout from Scotland teaches an American Scout the Highland Fling while a compatriot plays the bagpipe, and Scouts from Indonesia and India join in the fun. The music is attracting other Scouts. A Scout from Israel is approaching from the left, and Scouts from Jamaica, Canada, Lebanon, and France are climbing the hillside at the right.
A GOOD SIGN ALL OVER THE WORLD   1963

The collection of Rockwell paintings that toured the United States during the Bicentennial Year of 1976 was housed in a spectacularly decorated Mack trailer-truck. It covered 16,000 miles in seven months and was viewed by 280,000 people.

The permanent home of Norman Rockwell's Scout paintings is the Johnston National Scouting Museum, presented to the Boy Scouts of America by Gale F. Johnston, a Boy Scout executive board member of St. Louis, Missouri, in memory of his wife. The museum is located behind the National Office in North Brunswick, New Jersey.

The Traveling Exhibition

The reproductions of Norman Rockwell's Scout paintings on the preceding pages are the finest that modern engraving and printing processes are able to achieve. But they are still reproductions—not the real thing.

There is a great emotional difference between looking at a reproduction and looking at a Rockwell original—an experience which has a very special impact on the viewer.

But how can it be done?

With very few exceptions, the Rockwell Scout paintings in this book are the property of the Boy Scouts of America. Some of them are displayed on a rotating basis in the Johnston National Scouting Museum, located on the grounds of the National Office of the Boy Scouts of America in North Brunswick, New Jersey. Those paintings not on display at any given moment are stored in the vaults of the National Office, waiting for the day when a special Rockwell wing might be added to the museum.

But it is not always necessary to travel to New Jersey to

Every Rockwell painting has its own special appeal to the audience. Every Scout sees in practically every picture one of his own Scouting experiences. A Cub Scout who saw this painting, *"Can't Wait"* *(left),* said, "That's the way I looked the day I got my brother's Scout uniform and tried it on."

Even a partial collection of Norman's Scout paintings tells of the excitement of Scouting: the joy of the outdoor life, the pride of reaching another rank, the responsibilities of leadership, the spirit of world brotherhood.

view a Rockwell Scout painting. From time to time, Norman's paintings travel around the country for special displays in various locations on a temporary basis.

An especially ambitious undertaking was the Norman Rockwell Scout Painting Tour during the Bicentennial Year, when a selection of paintings insured for $1.5 million went on a 16,000-mile trip around America. This tour was made possible by the financial support of the Signal Companies, Inc., of Los Angeles, California; the generous loan, by Mack Trucks of Allentown, Pennsylvania, of a specially decorated Mack trailer-truck and a driver; and the help of public-spirited supporters and the local Scout council in each city visited.

The collection for this tour consisted of thirty-one of Norman's Scout paintings, packed like jewels in special velvet-lined containers and accompanied by display panels and lighting fixtures. In each of the fifteen cities where the pictures were exhibited, the closely guarded containers were unlocked, and the paintings carefully removed and hung on their panels, where they could be viewed by Scouts and the general public. The exhibition was mounted in a variety of places, among them an art museum, a convention hall, a municipal auditorium, a bank lobby, a shopping mall, and a department store. During its seven-month tour, this traveling exhibit was viewed by 280,000 people.

There is small chance that a major collection of Norman's Scout paintings will ever again travel around the country. From time to time, some of his paintings may be on loan exhibition in various communities. But if you really want to see Norman's Scout paintings, come to the Johnston National Scouting Museum in North Brunswick, New Jersey, and see them in their best possible setting, surrounded by memorabilia of Scouting from its beginnings to the present day.

Norman Rockwell's Boy Scout Calendars

Most of the color photographs of these paintings were taken specially for this book by George Roos

Index